TURNING HOLLOW FORMS

TURNING HOLLOW FORMS

TECHNIQUES AND PROJECTS

MARK SANGER

The Taunton Press

The Taunton Press
Inspiration for hands-on living®

The Taunton Press, Inc., 63 South Main Street
P.O. Box 5506, Newtown, CT 06470-5506
e-mail: tp@taunton.com

First published 2013 by Guild of Master Craftsman Publications Ltd
Castle Place, 166 High Street, Lewes, East Sussex BN7 1XU

Text © Mark Sanger, 2013
Copyright in the Work © GMC Publications Ltd, 2013

Library of Congress Cataloging-in-Publication Data
Sanger, Mark.
  Turning hollow forms : techniques and projects / Mark Sanger.
    pages cm
  ISBN 978-1-62710-027-4 (pbk.)
1. Turning (Lathe work) 2. Woodwork. I. Title.
  TT203.S36 2014
  684'.083--dc23

                    2013040162

Publisher: Jonathan Bailey
Production Manager: Jim Bulley
Managing Editor: Gerrie Purcell
Senior Project Editors: Cath Senker and Sara Harper
Editor: Nicola Hodgson
Managing Art Editor: Gilda Pacitti
Designers: Simon Goggin and Rob Janes
Photography: Mark Sanger and Anthony Bailey

Set in Gibson and Frutiger; color origination by GMC Reprographics
Printed and bound in China

Dedication
This book is dedicated to my late grandparents who shared with me their love of the countryside and the beauty of working with wood. Thank you to my mother Elaine for her unwavering support of my family and work. To my loving wife, Lizzie; you are always there supporting and encouraging me; and to Bethany and Bella, my loving, smart daughters, thank you for being my best critics and for making life such fun.

About Your Safety
Working wood is inherently dangerous. Using hand or power tools improperly or ignoring safety practices can lead to permanent injury or even death. Don't try to perform operations you learn about here (or elsewhere) unless you're certain they are safe for you. If something about an operation doesn't feel right, don't do it. Enjoy the craft, but keep safety foremost in your mind whenever you're in the shop.

Imperial/metric conversions
The emphasis in this book is on the techniques and processes required to make the projects. The measurements given are intended as a guide to give a sense of scale and you may adapt them according to your preference for using either metric or imperial systems. I use the metric system and, as conversion to imperial can introduce inaccuracies, I recommend you stick to one or the other and do not mix up the measurements.

CONTENTS

INTRODUCTION

Woodturning is a mesmerizing and tactile craft. The tools, techniques and theory may seem daunting initially – not to mention the unpredictable way in which wood reacts when worked. But do not be put off; beginners can readily learn woodturning techniques.

When I picked up my first copy of a woodturning magazine, I was hooked by the way in which a piece of wood could be turned so quickly from a rough blank to a bowl, spindle, box or hollow form. I was immediately drawn by the mystique of hollow-form turning; I thought, surely turning through such a small hole is beyond my reach? The wonderful work of Cindy Drozda, David Ellsworth, John Jordan, Mark Baker, Phil Irons, Stuart Mortimer and many others who have shared their work and skills through articles and books over the years inspired me along the enjoyable path of turning hollow forms. Many thanks go to all these masterful turners and the others, too many to mention, who have had such a huge influence on me. They inspired my decision to leave a full-time career in the police force to pursue woodturning as a way of life, and I have never looked back.

At first, when I started trying to produce work similar to my idols', I found it was not as easy as they made it look. My tooling was coming along alright, but I was amassing a sizable pile of distorted and cracked forms fit only for the fire. I realized that although it was important to learn the safe use of tools, I also needed to understand wood: how to process it, season it, and ultimately get the best from it. When I decided to start selling my work, I began to appreciate the importance of shape and form. It soon became apparent that no matter how proficient I became in using the tools and utilizing the wood, shape and form topped the list if I were to have any hope of selling my work for a price that reflected the time spent producing it.

The lessons I learned became the basis for the contents of this book. Everything you need to set you on the right path is included, from safe and efficient tool use, wood technology and seasoning to considerations of shape and form. Each subject is intertwined with the others and all are equally important. Having a sound understanding of each subject will provide you with a solid foundation for the turning of deep and hollow vessels.

There are hundreds of tools on the market. Here we discuss the individual categories of tools and the theory behind them. Although different tools may be produced by different manufacturers, the theory of use within their group will be the same. Remember that no tool on its own will produce a pleasing form: only understanding and practice can achieve this.

My grandfather would often say to me as I embarked on a new subject, "sort the wheat from the chaff." This ethos is how I work and how this book has been written. There will always be lessons to learn, skills to perfect, and more theory to absorb, but initially much of it is not critical for success and can often lead to confusion. Of course, like me, you will never stop learning. This is the most exciting part of the craft!

Work safely and enjoy the journey.
Happy turning!

Mark Sanger

HOW TO USE THIS BOOK

First, I cover the safety aspects of woodturning, tools, techniques, wood and seasoning, and shape and form, before setting out a series of projects. You may want to jump straight to the project section and start turning. If this is the case, you can simply utilize seasoned wood blanks. This will limit the size of the forms that can be turned, but all of the projects are equally suited to unseasoned or seasoned wood.

Please read the section on safety before anything else. You may have a good understanding of health and safety, but you should always refresh this knowledge. Woodturning is enjoyable but also inherently dangerous, so take care.

My advice is to read all the chapters in sequence initially and then to dip back into them as you start to turn the various projects. The theory has been kept to the essential minimum and therefore I believe all the chapters are relevant to you. You may be familiar with some of the subjects, but it is always good to look at how other people work so you can pick up fresh perspectives along the way.

If you want to jump straight to turning the projects, you should at least read the sections on tooling and form. However, if you want to select and process your own unseasoned wood, then understanding the section on wood first is essential.

The projects have been designed to be progressive, moving from turning enclosed forms then going on to hollow forms, eventually turning through a small entrance hole. Also included are projects showing how to achieve a hollow form using various methods, such as turning through the base or shoulder. Each project requires its own skill set to help you build upon your tooling skills and knowledge of wood and form.

As you work through the book and projects, take notes on how each project progresses and how the wood reacts; reflect on what you produced, how well it went, and any changes you might need to make for the next one. If you are unsure, dip back into the relevant chapter, and keep practicing and enjoying the process.

Finally, and most importantly, the one part of turning you cannot afford to get wrong is safety. Never become complacent, and frequently refresh your knowledge and safe working practices.

CHAPTER ONE

HEALTH AND SAFETY

Woodturning is a fun, relaxing and creative craft, but it is also inherently dangerous. There are many precautions that should be taken when using machinery or tools in the workshop. Always read the safety instructions that accompany the machines and tools you use. Work within your own limits, the limits of the machines and tools you are using, and the limits of the wood you are turning. Keep your workshop clean and tidy. Never forget that if you become complacent you may put yourself or others in harm's way, and this could result in serious injury or even death.

GOOD PRACTICE

There are inherent dangers in woodturning, but smart workshop practice will minimize the risks involved with the use of machinery and tools, storage of items, connection of items to electrical supply, spinning wood held on the lathe, the production of dust and also the use of finishes. This chapter sets out some practical pointers to help you work smartly and safely.

SETTING UP THE WORKSHOP

The photo above shows dangerous workshop practices you should avoid. The workshop needs to be set up so that you have clear space to work without trip hazards such as wiring running across the floor. Wood and equipment should be kept out of your working area. Items need to be stored and situated effectively and safely – you may need to organize racking, shelving and tables to facilitate this. Note that in the set-up on page 14, there are no trailing wires on the floor; items are up on the shelves out of the way, and there is clear floor space in front of the lathe so I can work without obstruction. Note also that items such as sharpening devices, tools and chucks are close to hand. The lathe is the center point and around it are the most commonly used items. The at-source dust-extraction system at the lathe is supplemented by ambient filtration units on the wall and ceiling to capture any dust not caught by the at-source extraction.

Dealing with dust is vital as it is hazardous to health; you are likely to need a few methods to deal with it to minimize your exposure. The at-source extraction system is one that captures dust as close to the work as possible; it is typically a drum- or bag-type system with a flexible hose arrangement. Various power and size options are available. Other methods include fixed ducting connected to a vacuum unit running around the workshop. Ambient extraction systems filter out dust that becomes airborne, and they do not need to cost the earth. Hook up with a trusted supplier so you can explore options suitable for your workshop and needs.

Note also the wooden tool rack on the lathe. This is where I place all the tools I need for my current project so I do not need to stop and reach over to the tool rack.

LIGHTING

Good lighting is vital. Strip or fluorescent lights are great for general lighting, but may cause a strobing effect on rotating lathe work. Directional lighting not only helps you direct lighting where you need it, but also stops the strobing effects that occur with strip lights. Here you can see some directional LED lights under a shelf and also a flexible magnetic light.

PROTECTIVE EQUIPMENT

It is necessary to wear protective equipment not only to minimize exposure to dust but also to flying debris. Safety glasses are often used to protect the eyes, but these do not protect the face. The better route in my opinion is to use a face shield – this not only offers better eye protection, but also better face and brow protection. This should be used in conjunction with a suitable face mask to minimize dust inhalation. The best option – although it is a more expensive one – is to buy a powered respirator system that is integral to a full face shield, as seen in the main picture here. You will need to remember to keep it charged up.

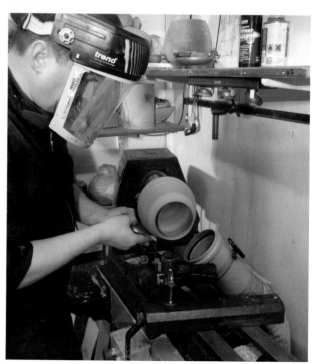

TURNING HOLLOW FORMS

SHARPENING

Keep sharpening simple by using a 6-in. (150mm) bench grinder with a rise-and-tilt table and fingernail jig on the fine grit wheel. It is set on a shelf and at a height that is easy to use and minimizes the need to bend over to view what I am doing.

WORK AREA

I have a clean work area for final finishing if required, or an area where I can enhance work further. The use of finishes can expose you to potentially harmful chemicals. Only use them in a well-ventilated area to minimize exposure to vapor and use special masks too as required. Remember to minimize exposure to the skin and wear special gloves if required.

TOOLS

The tools are stored securely in a rack where they cannot fall out and are nearby for when I need them. Pipe clips are simple and inexpensive. I also use magnetic racks for smaller items. Remember to keep cutting tools sharp so they do their job properly, and always treat them with respect.

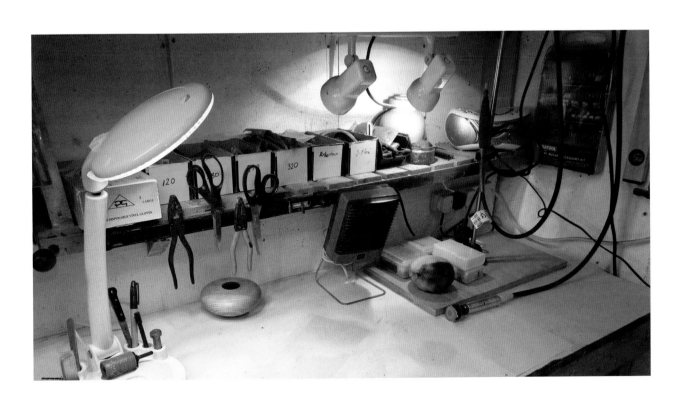

SPEED OF WORK ON THE LATHE

It is important to work at the right speed for the size, condition and type of wood you are turning. Here are two charts that will help guide you when selecting speeds. Remember, the larger the work, the lower the speed required. Look at the condition of the wood to check for faults that could compromise the integrity of the piece: bark can fly off, or cracks and fissures could be bigger and deeper than you might think and risk the piece exploding on you. You need to make an honest value call as to whether you should be working with it. If you choose to go ahead, assess the risks and try to minimize them.

FACEPLATE SPEEDS

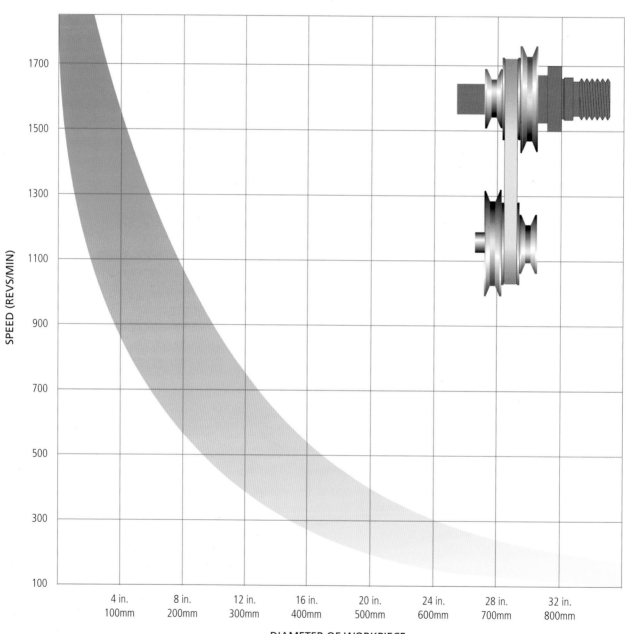

SPEED (REVS/MIN)

1700
1500
1300
1100
900
700
500
300
100

| 4 in.
100mm | 8 in.
200mm | 12 in.
300mm | 16 in.
400mm | 20 in.
500mm | 24 in.
600mm | 28 in.
700mm | 32 in.
800mm |

DIAMETER OF WORKPIECE

SPINDLE SPEEDS

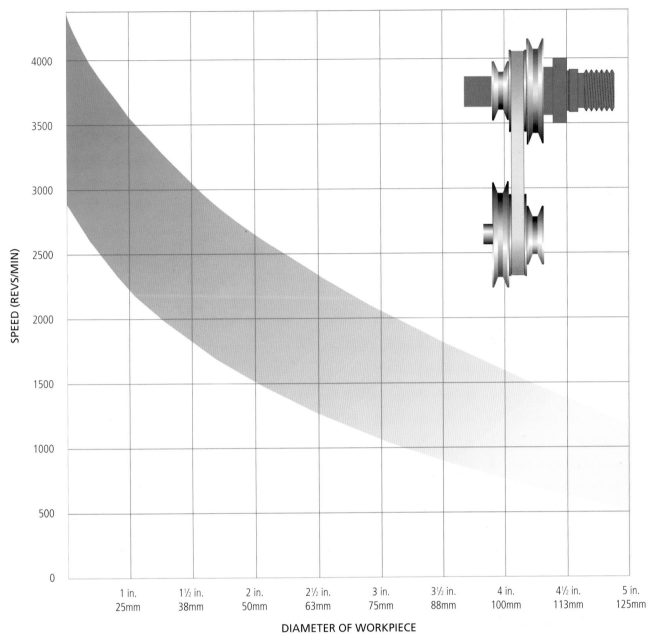

SPEED (REVS/MIN)

4000

3500

3000

2500

2000

1500

1000

500

0

| 1 in. | 1½ in. | 2 in. | 2½ in. | 3 in. | 3½ in. | 4 in. | 4½ in. | 5 in. |
| 25mm | 38mm | 50mm | 63mm | 75mm | 88mm | 100mm | 113mm | 125mm |

DIAMETER OF WORKPIECE

SAFE WORKING

In conclusion, my advice is to always follow the manufacturer's instructions when using tools, equipment and finishes. If you are in doubt about a process, seek professional advice so you can work as safely as possible. I have touched on only a few potential hazards and made suggestions that will help you, but do ensure that you think safe and work smart at all times.

Even professionals can make mistakes. A combination of things went wrong to cause this bowl to fracture and explode – part of it ended up in the ceiling of my workshop.

CHAPTER TWO

WOOD

Wood is a beautiful and tactile material. It is still unrivaled
by many modern materials due to its inherent beauty and
characteristics when worked. The sheer volume of species,
grain patterns and colors means there is an almost endless
variation and supply for us to turn. Many species take
hundreds of years to mature and, with no two sections of
tree being the same, we should be aware that we are taking
part in a very special process. For me, this is why I find
working with wood so satisfying; I am always excited
to see what lies below the bark.

WOOD: THE BASICS

The variety of species, inherent colors and grain patterns of wood make it a beautiful and exciting material to work with. It is readily available from many sources: from friends, neighbors, farmers and tree surgeons to small-scale wood mills. It is possible to purchase pre-cut seasoned bowl and spindle blanks that offer certain benefits; however, these are generally only available up to a thickness of 4 in. (100mm), which can be restrictive for turning deep or hollow vessels.

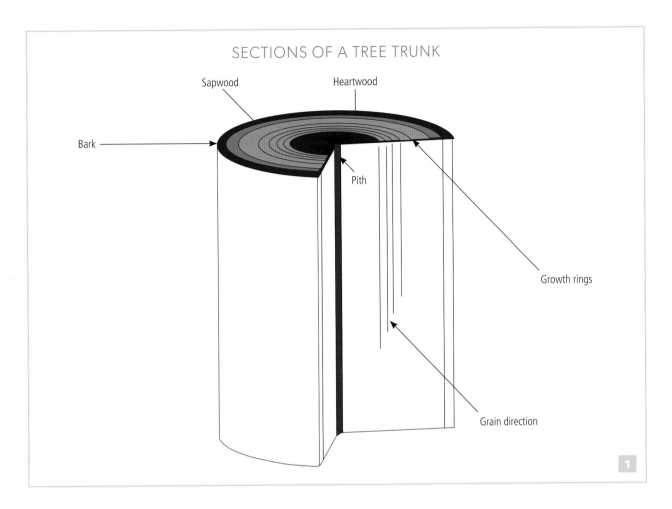

SECTIONS OF A TREE TRUNK

Sapwood

Heartwood

Bark

Pith

Growth rings

Grain direction

Having the knowledge to select, turn and season the wood that we have collected allows us full control from start to finished project. It is satisfying and cost-effective to process, turn and season your own wood; while it might seem initially daunting, it is in fact a relatively simple process.

There are many books available covering wood technology in much greater depth than we can here; these are listed in the bibliography (see page 163). Within the context of this book, I will share the methods used in my work so you can select, turn and season projects successfully with the minimum of fuss. There is a foundation of theory needed for this, but I have, where possible, kept this to the minimum practically required for success.

BELOW THE BARK

Wood is the material harvested from trees; it is constructed from millions of elongated cells that grow in line with the pith, and this in turn gives the direction of grain. The growth of a tree is measured by the number of rings counted through the cross-section of its trunk. The rings are made up of early and late growth, the first being lighter in color and lower in density than the late-growth rings.

Early growth is produced during the warmer seasons; late growth is produced at a slower rate in fall to early winter and continues until the dormant phase in midwinter when the tree all but goes into hibernation. The warmth of the following spring triggers the cycle into action again, when nutrients are drawn into the tree via the root and leaf structures in what we will describe here as water.

This water fills both the cell walls and the voids inside and around them. The water contained within the structure of the cell walls is known as bound water. The remaining liquid being held inside and around the cells is known as free water. Free water is most evident when it sprays out from a freshly cut log being turned on a lathe. The loss of this free water has no effect on the seasoning of the wood other than it has to evaporate before the bound water is released from the cells. Bound water and the speed with which it evaporates has a direct effect on the wood structure during seasoning. If this moisture loss is not controlled, then the result is often failure in the structure of the wood, frequently seen as checking and cracks. **1** shows a simplified cross-section of a tree including grain direction, pith, heartwood and sapwood, and is a good place for us to start.

CLASSIFICATION

Wood is classified into two categories: hardwoods and softwoods. Hardwoods are generally deciduous and are slower-growing than softwoods, which are evergreen and have needle-like foliage. Hardwoods include oak, ash and maple; softwoods include yew, pine, redwood and cedar.

Both softwoods and hardwoods can be turned for vessels with stunning grain effects. **2** shows a hardwood spalted beech (*Fagus sylvatica*) hollow form turned by George Watkins; **3** shows a softwood yew (*Taxus baccata*) form turned by George Foweraker.

GRAIN ORIENTATION

The orientation of the grain refers to the direction in which the grain is aligned to be joined, laid or cut. In the case of woodturning it refers to the direction in which grain is aligned in relation to the spindle axis of the lathe or, more simply, its direction in relation to the lathe bed.

Two methods of orientation on the lathe are cross grain and parallel (or end) grain. Each orientation is approached differently for the initial processing of blanks and for turning on the lathe. **4** shows both of these methods and how they are mounted on the lathe.

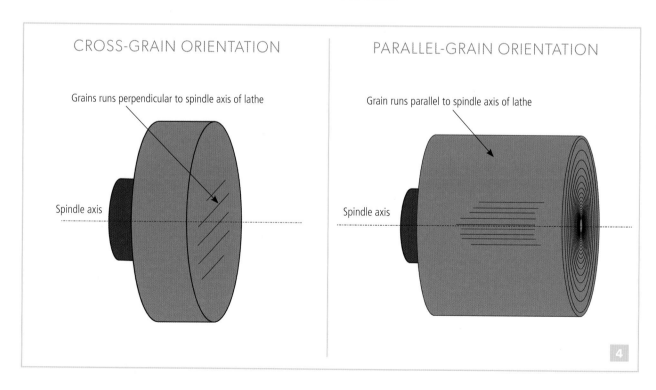

CROSS-GRAIN ORIENTATION

Grains runs perpendicular to spindle axis of lathe

Spindle axis

PARALLEL-GRAIN ORIENTATION

Grain runs parallel to spindle axis of lathe

Spindle axis

CROSS GRAIN

When the grain runs perpendicular to the spindle axis or lathe bed, it is said to be cross grain. This is most commonly used for the turning of bowls and platters. The turning of unseasoned cross-grain orientated wood and the amount of movement induced during seasoning can be problematic when turning deep or hollow vessels. As such, the most common method of grain orientation for deep and hollow forms is known as parallel grain, when the wood grain runs in line with the spindle axis of the lathe. With experience, cross-grain orientated wood can be utilized for the turning of deeper forms, but here its use is limited to that of turning seasoned wood; while restrictive in thickness, it can be used to great effect. **5** shows a cross-grain walnut form, revealing how cross-grain orientation including both the dark heartwood and lighter sapwood can be maximized to great effect. To achieve this, a seasoned slab of walnut was cut from a board to include a percentage of both sapwood and heartwood.

PARALLEL GRAIN

When the wood grain runs in line with the spindle axis of the lathe, this is parallel grain; it is often referred to as end-grain turning. The main benefits compared to cross grain are that the amount of movement during seasoning is greatly reduced and gives the benefit of turning vessels straight to finish from unseasoned wood with little or no degradation of form. Another benefit of parallel-grain wood is that the amount of movement induced during seasoning of forms that are initially rough-turned for later finishing is also reduced.

Parallel-grain wood is processed in two ways for turning on the lathe: pith included and pith excluded. As with cross-grain turning, the blank can be processed from the tree to include or exclude sapwood and hardwood. **6** shows a cherry (*Prunus*) lidded form that has been turned with the pith offset slightly from the spindle axis of the lathe; the heartwood shows through the central sapwood, adding interest to the piece.

HANDY HINT

The choice of grain orientation will affect not only the aesthetics of the finished project but also the way in which it is turned. Owing to the availability of seasoned wood, tall vessels will often be produced using parallel grain stock, while small forms offer themselves for turning from seasoned cross-grain stock. Whichever option you choose, the quality of the lumber is a major consideration, so select the best available to you.

5

6

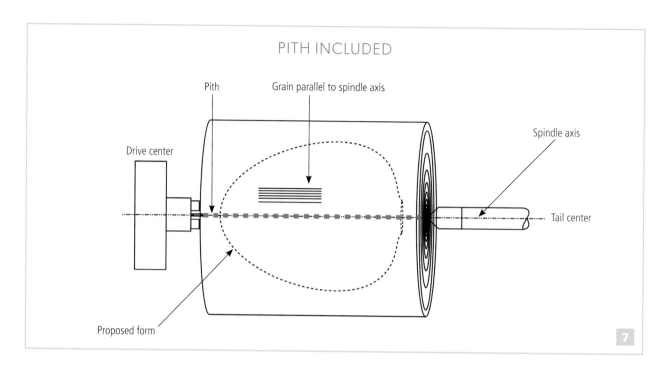

PITH INCLUDED

PITH INCLUDED

Pith

Grain parallel to spindle axis

Spindle axis

Drive center

Tail center

Proposed form

7

PITH INCLUDED

In **7**, pith included is shown. This is when the pith is aligned centrally with the spindle axis of the lathe. It gives the option to turn small branchwood as well as deeper vessels from larger logs where the only processing required is to cut the log to length. A drawback is that if seasoning is not controlled, the wood is susceptible to cracks radiating from the pith to the outer edge. **8** shows this in a small slice from the end of a branch; this has occurred due to the outside of the log drying rapidly, resulting in the internal saturated fibers pushing out until the fibers fail and the log splits. This is why the pith-excluded method, discussed next, is often the preferred method of processing for turning deep vessels. Despite this, if seasoning is controlled when utilizing pith-included stock, a high rate of success is achieved. This is a method I have employed myself for many years.

PITH EXCLUDED

Pith excluded (as in **10a** opposite) shows the cross-section of a large trunk on the face of which blanks are drawn. It also shows how these blanks are orientated on the lathe. **9** shows a spalted silver birch (*Betula pendula*) hollow form turned from such a blank. This method of processing allows for several blanks to be cut from large sections that would otherwise be too heavy to load or turn on the lathe. This produces a more forgiving structure for seasoning, thus reducing the chance of failure through cracking. This makes it the most favorable option if we have the tools to process the wood further than just cutting to length. Diagrams **10b** and **10c** on pages 28–29 show processing diagrams for pith excluded and cross grain.

8

9

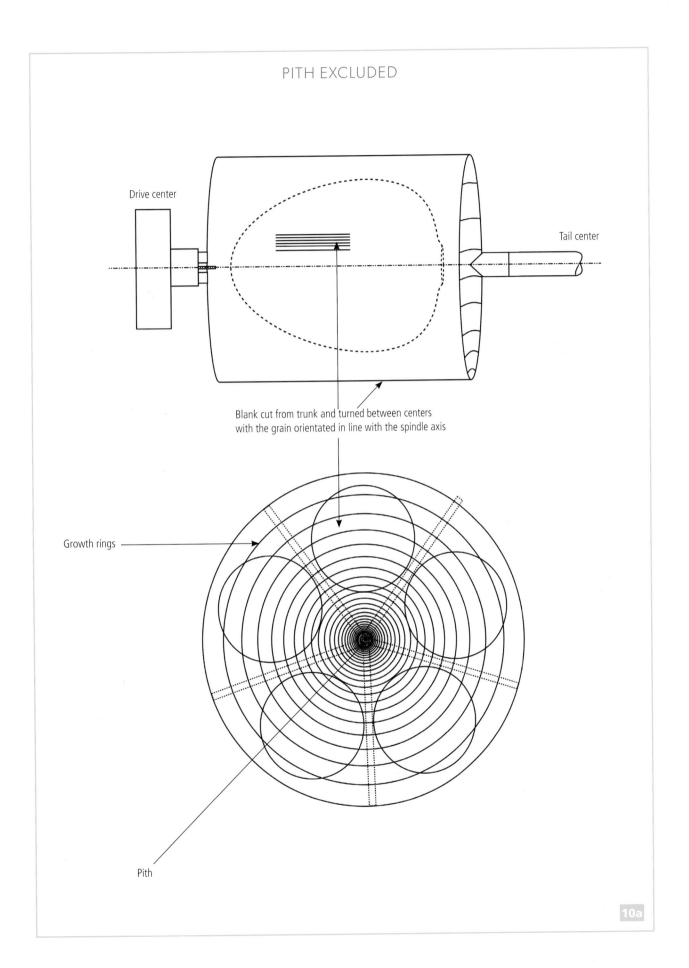

Drive center

Tail center

Blank cut from trunk and turned between centers
with the grain orientated in line with the spindle axis

Growth rings

Pith

10a

PROCESSING DIAGRAMS: PITH EXCLUDED

Cut trunk or log to length

Divide into sections to accommodate diameter of blanks

Dividing cuts

Cut away corners, producing a hexagon

Alternatively cut into the round

10b

PROCESSING DIAGRAMS: CROSS GRAIN

Cut log or trunk to length followed by a sectioning down through the middle, with
any material in the round being appropriately and safely supported

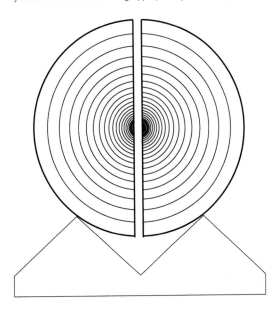

Place flat down and cut blanks to the round or cut off corners

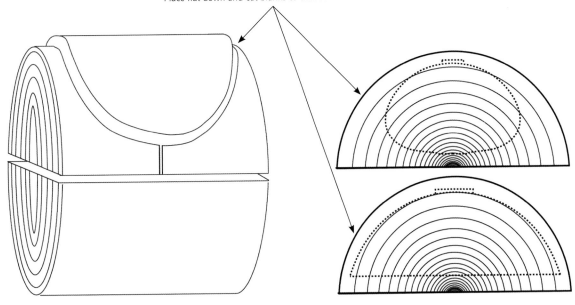

THE FIRST CUT

On being felled, the sap of a tree starts to escape through evaporation via the side and end grain of the wood structure. This moisture loss causes shrinking and movement within the wood fibers. If not controlled during seasoning, this can result in failure, often first noticeable through cracking.

The amount of shrinkage and movement in wood during seasoning relates to several factors, including: the species and growing conditions, the grain structure, and where and how it has been processed from the tree. **11** shows a cross-section of a tree with concentric growth rings and the pith aligned centrally. Labeled are the mean percentages and directions of shrinkage for lumber from saturated to seasoned. Knowing these directions of shrinkage helps us to understand what happens in our projects as they season and why they may fail.

- Tangential shrinkage: occurs perpendicular to the grain and parallel to the growth rings.

- Radial shrinkage: occurs perpendicular to the growth rings.

- Longitudinal shrinkage: occurs along the length of the grain, is minimal and as such can be discounted.

MEAN SHRINKAGE IN WOOD

Tangential shrinkage 8%

Radial shrinkage 4%

Longitudinal shrinkage 0.1%

11

TANGENTIAL SHRINKAGE

After seasoning a cross-grain vessel, tangential shrinkage is most noticeable. For example, a bowl turned straight to finished size will move to a mean of 8% tangentially, the effect being that the wood moves down and away from the pith. This is fine if you want to produce a warped bowl, but if not, the blank has to be rough-turned to leave enough thickness for later finishing. **12** shows a small rough-turned cherry cross-grain bowl, clearly showing the resulting tangential movement during seasoning.

12

RADIAL SHRINKAGE

Radial shrinkage occurs to a mean of 4% of the diameter. A log with perfectly concentric growth rings and the pith aligned as in **11** would in theory during seasoning shrink consistently by 4% of its diameter while remaining perfectly round. Such a log, of course, does not exist, but through careful selection we can start from a stable foundation. The results of careful wood selection can be seen in **13** and **13a**, which show a 12-in. (300mm)-diameter ash (*Fraxinus excelsior*) bowl, rough-turned and fully seasoned, ready for finishing. The movement induced was negligible in comparison to the cross-grain bowl in **12** and shows the stability of such orientated well-chosen stock.

With a pith-excluded blank, only part of the whole is utilized and therefore only part of the shrinkage occurs during seasoning. Radial shrinkage occurs parallel with the growth rings, resulting in the final form being slightly oval in shape. The degree of oval induced relates to how far from the pith the blank is cut – the farther away, the less the movement. If you decide to later fit a lid, you will need to first rough-turn for remounting and finishing once seasoned. A blank processed adjacent to the pith will produce an oval form with a bulge closest to the pith. **14** shows the resulting movement for pith included and pith excluded as well as a cross-grain section.

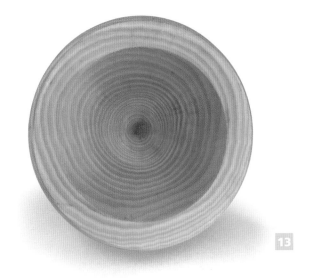

13

13a

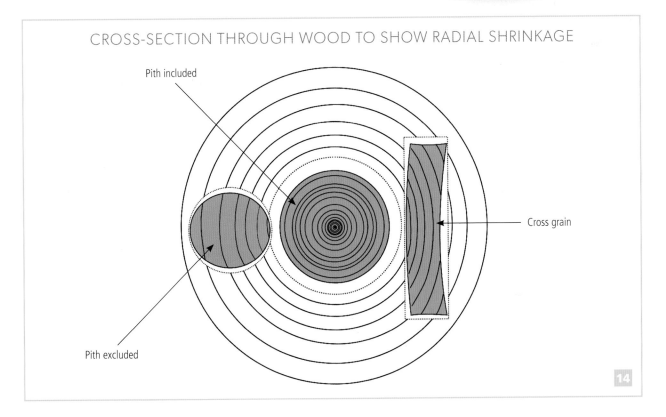

CROSS-SECTION THROUGH WOOD TO SHOW RADIAL SHRINKAGE

Pith included

Cross grain

Pith excluded

14

MOVEMENT

Shrinkage and movement in wood are not constants; any two pieces cut from the same tree can react differently during seasoning. Interlocking grain and the use of 'normal' or 'reaction' wood, discussed later, can also affect the end result.

Specific species have certain characteristics, but the listing of shrinkage rates for each, I believe, is of little value compared to a list of species in order of ease for working and seasoning. We can then initially select the woods that are forgiving and move down the list as experience is gained.

Any sound wood can be turned and seasoned with relative ease. Faster-growing woods of lower density such as sycamore (*Acer pseudoplatanus*) have flexible structures and are forgiving when worked and seasoned. Slow-growing dense woods such as yew (*Taxus baccata*) have fibers that are less pliable, requiring more attention when worked and seasoned. If poor-quality stock is selected and/or seasoning is not controlled, then most woods will fail; some will just fail more quickly than others.

The table below lists woods in order of ease of use via a color scheme of greens, orange and red, with the most forgiving species listed within the green section.

Species table

Species	Working properties	Seasoning
European sycamore (*Acer pseudoplatanus*)	Works well	Dries quickly, seasons well/forgiving
Rock maple/Hard maple (*Acer saccharum* and *A. nigrum*)	Works well	Dries quickly, seasons well/forgiving
European beech (*Fagus sylvatica*)	Works well	Dries quickly, needs care when seasoning
American beech (*Fagus grandifolia*)	Works well	Dries quickly, seasons slowly
European ash (*Fraxinus excelsior*)	Works well	Dries quickly, seasons slowly
American ash (*Fraxinus Americana*)	Works well	Dries quickly, seasons slowly
European walnut (*Juglans regia*)	Works well	Dries slowly, liable to checking if not seasoned slowly
European cherry (*Prunus avium*)	Works well	Dries quickly, liable to movement, checking and splitting if not seasoned slowly
American cherry (*Prunus serotina*)	Works well	Dries quickly and is prone to movement and checking. Seasons slowly.
Yew (*Taxus baccata*)	Works well if straight-grained	Dries quickly but is liable to degrading and checking and distortion. Seasons slowly.
Apple (*Malus sylvestris*)	Works well	Dries slowly, liable to movement and checking. Seasons slowly.
Pear (*Pyrus communis*)	Works well	Dries slowly, liable to movement and checking. Seasons slowly.
English elm (*Ulmus procera*)	Difficult to work	Dries quickly with high chance of movement, checking and splitting. Seasons slowly.
European oak (*Quercus robur*)	Works satisfactorily; checks and splits	Slow-drying, liable to large amount of movement, Seasons very slowly.
American white oak (*Quercus alba*)	Works well	Dries slowly, difficult to season and liable to checking and splitting. Seasons very slowly.

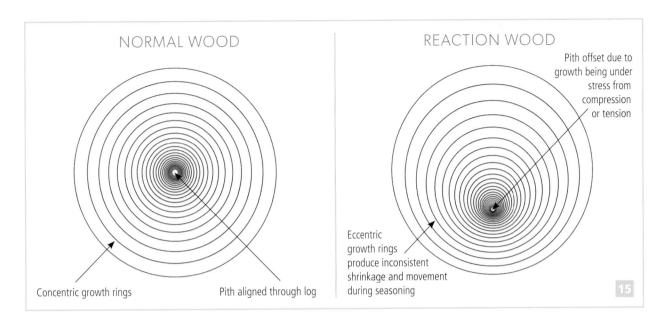

NORMAL WOOD

Concentric growth rings

Pith aligned through log

REACTION WOOD

Pith offset due to growth being under stress from compression or tension

Eccentric growth rings produce inconsistent shrinkage and movement during seasoning

`15`

SELECTING STOCK

Choosing the right stock is essential, so what should you look for in a branch, log or larger section for your blanks? To know this you need to understand the difference between 'normal' and 'reaction' wood.

Normal wood grows under consistent low-stress conditions of vertical direction, as in the trunk and vertical growing branches of a tree. Such growing conditions produce a stable structure with a perfect section of normal wood, as represented in `15`. Here you can see the growth rings are concentric with the pith aligned centrally through its length. It is, of course, rare to find such a perfect section due to growing conditions, but aim as close to this as possible when selecting your stock.

Reaction wood is wood subjected to the stress of compression or tension, such as the trunk of a leaning tree, one subjected to high winds, or the wood found in the more horizontal growing branches. `15` also shows a representation of reaction wood.

When seasoned, such a piece of reaction wood will induce inconsistent shrinkage. The result of this is seen in `16`, a thin-walled ash (*Fraxinus excelsior*) form that was turned from such a cross-section. While the wood was taken from the same tree as the bowl in `13` and `13a`, with both forms orientated the same for turning, the variation is evident. The structure within the hollow form has bulged to the top right with cracks appearing near the rim, unlike the bowl, which has remained near perfectly round with no sign of failure. The perfect cross-section does not exist, but in `17a` we can see normal wood suitable for our needs and in `17b`, reaction wood, which is unsuitable.

In short, if you steer clear of reaction wood, select good-quality normal wood, devoid of cracks, branches and other inclusions, your rate of success will be high. There are, of course, exceptions to the rule; as you gain experience in thin-wall turning you may want to experiment with using reaction wood for dramatic and unpredictable effects.

`16`

`17a`

`17b`

PROCESSING BLANKS

There are many tools available to process wood, from a bow saw for small branches to axes, splitting wedges, chain saws and band saws for larger sections. It is not my intention here to cover the specific use of each tool and/or machine. If you already have a chain saw and/or band saw, take the greatest of care; I would urge you to attend a suitable training course with a qualified instructor. Improper use of any tool can result in serious injury or even death. Your local directory or tool company will have details of where such courses are available. While you may feel this is yet another cost you can do without, it is far better this than crying over spilled blood when you have lost a body part through improper use. Always be fully compliant in all current safety instructions and legislation and be in possession of (and use) all the required personal safety equipment – it is of no use hanging on a hook in your workshop.

Here I will show how both parallel-grain and cross-grain blanks are processed from a branch or trunk; you will be able to use this information to process your blanks.

Another option that incurs a relatively small cost for the yield of material processed is to use the services of a sawyer. This gives greater control over the process, enabling specific characteristics such as grain pattern or the inclusion of both heartwood and sapwood. This option is not available with pre-cut blanks, as the process is about maximum yield. **18** shows a local sawyer cutting to length some rounds of ash for hollow forms; **19** shows a large band saw being set to cut slabs from a trunk.

PARALLEL-GRAIN BLANKS FROM THE ROUND

The diagram below shows the stages and cuts – indicated in red – for the processing of pith-excluded blanks for the turning of deep vessels such as vases and hollow forms. Movement induced during seasoning in such blanks is greatly reduced compared to that of cross-grain alignment. This is the method I mainly employ for all of my deep vessel and hollow forms produced from unseasoned wood.

Pith excluded

Cut trunk or log to length

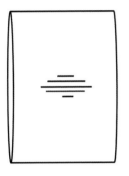

Divide into two

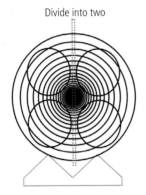

Further divide for individual blanks

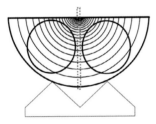

Cut away corners to produce a hexagon

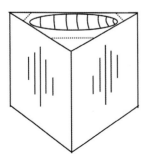

Alternatively cut into the round

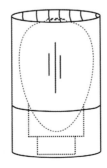

CROSS-GRAIN BLANKS FROM THE ROUND

The diagram below shows the stages and cuts – indicated in red – for processing cross-grain blanks for bowls or cross-grain hollow forms.

Cross-grain orientation, as we know, will induce the most movement during seasoning and as such is mostly employed for bowl turning. Seasoned cross-grain blanks for smaller projects will be stable and can be used for forms up to 4 in. (100mm) thick. This is a good place to start for small forms where the dramatic grain pattern of a cross-grain blank is desired.

Cross grain

Cut the log or trunk to length followed by a sectioning down through the middle, with any material being in the round being appropriately and safely supported

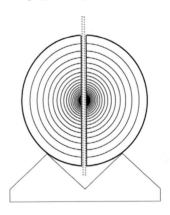

Place flat face down and cut blanks to the round. If you do not have the saw to do this, then cutting off the corners to produce a hexagon is sufficient for turning

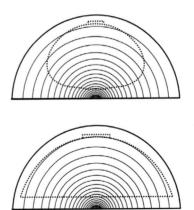

SEASONING

Now let us consider the methods employed to season thin-walled and rough-turned forms. You will hear of many ways to speed up the seasoning process, from boiling the wood, using microwave cookers, to soaking the wood in chemicals and home-mixed solutions. You may want to try these later; while they may reduce the seasoning time to some degree, they are not covered in this book. I have found that allowing nature to slowly do her thing yields the best results with the minimum of fuss.

The time it takes to season a wood varies from species to species: a thin-walled form can season within 1–2 weeks, while a thicker roughed form can take 4–8 months – **20** shows a stack of ash (*Fraxinus excelsior*) trunks ready for processing and roughing out. After a short time of roughing out blanks and producing thin-walled forms you will build up a good supply and, as the first batch seasons and as long as you keep roughing more forms, the cycle will become self-perpetuating. If you want immediate results, start with smaller seasoned blanks as you wait for your main stock to season.

As we know, wood contains moisture when cut from the tree. This moisture reduces over time through evaporation until it equals the level of moisture within the atmosphere. At this point it is known as being in a "state of equilibrium." Most turnings will end up in a home or other similar indoor environment, so the wood in our projects must be seasoned to match its final environment; if not, there is a high possibility it will crack.

Knowledge of exact percentage rates of moisture in woods is not required; we only need to know when the wood is seasoned or not. Wood is porous by nature and is known as being hygroscopic; this means the fibers will soak up or expel moisture in direct relation to the moisture contained in the atmosphere. This is why a wooden door will swell up and jam in the damp season yet shrink and close in the dry season.

The thickness of a piece of wood has a direct relationship to the time it takes to season; the thicker the piece, the longer it will take. As a guide, it is said it takes one year for every inch thickness of wood plus a year to fully season. Therefore, a 4-in. (100mm) piece would take five years to season in a normal air drying environment; this is more a "guesstimate" than an accurate guide as it very much depends on the characteristics of the species being seasoned; a dense wood will take far longer than a fast-growing, open-grain wood to season.

To season successfully we simply slow down the rate of moisture release to a level that allows the fibers to shrink and relax without failing until it equals the moisture content in its surrounding environment. Later in the chapter the specific methods I use to season are discussed (see page 38). Before this, let us look at the wall thickness of a form and how this relates to the process of seasoning.

WALL THICKNESS

Consistency is the main consideration in relation to wall thickness for successful seasoning; wall thickness coupled with controlled seasoning are closely related and should be considered as one. An inconsistent wall thickness will result in inconsistent shrinkage and is a major factor in a form cracking when seasoned.

Fast-growing woods, for example, European sycamore *(Acer pseudoplatanus)* or maple *(Acer saccharum)*, are more forgiving when seasoned compared to slower-growing dense species; the latter as a result are more susceptible to cracking if wall thickness and seasoning are not controlled and consistent. **21** shows a form with consistent wall thickness and a second shows where the areas are most likely to be either thick or thin, resulting in uneven shrinkage and movement.

CONSISTENT AND INCONSISTENT
WALL THICKNESSES

Consistent wall thickness resulting in even movement during seasoning

Areas susceptible to being turned too thin during hollowing

Inconsistent wall thickness resulting in uneven movement can cause failure during seasoning

21

WALL THICKNESS FOR A THIN-WALLED FORM

A thin wall gives the option of a vessel being turned straight to finish, greatly reducing the time of seasoning compared to that of thicker rough-turned forms to the many years required for a thick slab of wood.

The general rule in a thin-walled vessel is to turn the wall thickness to ⅛–¼ in. (3–6mm). This applies to both cross-grain and parallel-grain forms and allows the structure of the wall to remain flexible, reducing the chance of cracking. If, however, the wall is ¼ in. (6mm) thick at the rim then it should be ¼ in. (6mm) thick in the base, so have a final check of thickness and refine if needed before finishing your project. A slight variation will not have any real effect with controlled seasoning, but aim for the most consistent results with every piece, especially when turning slow-growing lumber.

WALL THICKNESS FOR A ROUGH-TURNED FORM

There are two reasons you may decide to rough-turn a form: if you want to add a lid the wood has to be fully seasoned and stable to achieve a good fit; otherwise, you may prefer the precision of the piece being perfectly round compared to the slight movement induced when turning to finish in one go.

WALL THICKNESS FOR A ROUGH-TURNED FORM WITH PARALLEL GRAIN

The wall thickness for a rough-turned form with parallel grain, whether pith included or excluded, should be around ½ in. (12mm) up to 8 in. (200mm) diameter. This will leave more than enough material for finishing after seasoning, as long as normal wood has been chosen. The wall can be turned thicker the larger the form, but I have never had a need to turn thicker than 1 in. (25mm) for forms up to 14 in. (350mm) in diameter and 14 in. (350mm) high; as long as the wall is consistent, the only variable is the amount of time it will take to season.

WALL THICKNESS FOR A ROUGH-TURNED FORM WITH CROSS GRAIN

For a rough-turned cross-grain form, the wall thickness should be 15% of the form diameter. So a 12-in. (300mm)-diameter form wall thickness will be 1¾ in. (45mm), leaving enough material for finishing to the round once seasoned. If turning to a thin wall, the same ⅛–¼ in. (3–6mm) applies.

HOW TO SEASON

Successful seasoning comes from controlling the speed of moisture release from the wood fibers. To achieve this we simply create a microclimate in which our project is placed to control this moisture loss. Large-scale kilns are used commercially. However, the items required for our needs are little more than finishing oil, a plastic bag, some newspaper or a commercially produced liquid end-grain sealer. I choose not to use the latter as it is more time-consuming, messy and expensive compared to recycling a plastic bag. However, all are discussed here and you can decide on your preferred method.

SEASONING ROUGH-TURNED FORMS

Check the wall thickness before removing your project from the lathe and refine if needed. Weigh the item and write this information and the date onto the waste area with a permanent marker.

Produce a microclimate in one of the following ways:

PLASTIC SHOPPING BAG

Place your project into a plastic shopping bag, folding over the top to stop moisture escaping (there is no need to tie it). For large forms or quantities, you can use a garbage bag. Either place the forms together in the bag or, if seasoning bowls, stack them on top of each other with props between each one to aid air circulation. Finally, slide the bag over the top, tucking it in around the base to protect from drafts. **22** shows a deep vessel in a plastic bag, ready for the details to be recorded.

Store or stack the forms in an accessible place. Take the forms out of the bag every two to three days. You will feel moisture has condensed on the inside wall of the bag. Turn the bag inside out and place the forms back inside, sealing as before. Repeat the process until the internal walls of the bag are dry. At this stage, leave the form/s in the bag but leave the top open, allowing the remaining moisture to escape slowly while being protected from excessive drafts.

Weigh the project every two to three weeks, recording the weight in a notebook. Leave in the open bag for several weeks, after which it can be removed and placed in a cool, draft-free location in your workshop. Continue to weigh. Once the weight has stabilized for several weeks, it is seasoned to the environment. Place in a cool location within your home and allow it to acclimatize for a week, after which the form can be finish-turned.

PAPER

An alternative method is to wrap each project in at least three layers of newspaper or similar, holding it in place with masking tape. Write the date, project and weight onto this. Weigh every two weeks as before until stable and continue, at which point again acclimatize the form to your home and finish-turn as before. **23** shows a project using this method being weighed and details recorded.

Wrapped project.

Once wrapped, label your project with name, date and weight.

COMMERCIALLY MADE END-GRAIN SEALER

There are many makes of liquid end-grain sealer/wax available, and all are suitable for the job. Unlike the blocks of solid paraffin wax available that have to be heated before applying, the liquid varieties can simply be applied with a brush without the fire risk associated with melting a solid block of wax. Simply paint onto the end grain of your projects and store in a cool area in the workshop, record the date and weight on to the project and continue as before. **24** shows a parallel-grain hollow form painted in end-grain sealer.

SEASONING THIN-WALLED VESSELS

Apply several generous coats of a thin finishing or food-safe oil, depending upon the intended use, both inside and out, wiping away any excess. The oil should be thin enough to allow it to soak into the fibers of the wood and not sit on top sealing the surface, or the moisture will be trapped and unable to escape. Lemon oil or general finishing oil are my preferred products for this purpose. Lemon oil dries to a matte finish, which in turn allows for a second oil specific to your desired finish to be applied after a couple of weeks or for the form to be buffed and sealed with a wax finish once fully seasoned. Place the form in an open plastic bag for two to three weeks, as in **25**, to prevent excessive moisture evaporation. Once the weight has stabilized, introduce the form into your home as before for a couple of weeks.

Seasoning really is simple and pain-free, especially if you build on a sound foundation from the start. Remember that the initial wood selection, consistency of wall thickness during the turning of the forms, and controlled seasoning all help to maximize success. Lack of patience is the cause of most failures through cracking, so take your time.

Painting with end-grain sealer.

Form left in open plastic bag.

CHAPTER THREE

TOOLS

Choosing the right tools and machinery is a daunting task; the sheer volume and variety available can be confusing. In this chapter the tools and machines are broken down into basic groups and how these best apply to our needs for turning hollow forms. Using the knowledge here you will be able to make sound decisions when purchasing the tools and machinery for your workshop, whether you are just setting up or have been turning for a while and want to start turning hollow forms.

HOLLOWING TOOLS

In this section I will show you the various types of hollowing tools available, with pointers on how and when to use them. No tool – no matter how much it costs – will make you a better turner; only practice will. My advice is to buy a limited range of good-quality tools from a reputable manufacturer, learn to use them well, and have fun turning.

LATHES

There are many lathes available of differing sizes and prices. Typically, the bigger the lathe you have, the more mass you have, and the bigger capacity you have at your disposal. That said, lathes usually increase in cost as they get bigger and, of course, take up more space. Which size you opt to buy is likely to be dictated by what you intend to make, the space available in the workshop, and your budget. Don't worry, though, as all the lathes I have ever come across have been suitable for turning hollow forms.

This book is not a treatise on what lathe I think you should buy. It is most important to consider your posture and stance and work comfortably in a position that feels right for you without causing pain in the back, arms or anywhere else. If you need to bend or twist over the lathe bed it could lead to discomfort in the short term or more serious problems in the long term.

I like to keep as straight a back as possible without bending, with feet shoulder-width apart and knees slightly bent. Therefore, lathe height and how you access the work are important considerations.

Find a lathe that will enable you to work in a comfortable position when hollowing and avoid you bending over the lathe. This might mean having a lathe that has a swiveling headstock, a headstock that will move along the lathe bed so you can alter its position to allow access for hollowing, or one that has a short enough lathe bed that you can stand at the end of it.

If you have a lathe with a fixed headstock position and a long lathe bed, you are likely to have to reach over, bend over or adjust your turning stance in order to work on hollow forms. This can be done successfully – just be aware of how you move your body and remember to turn comfortably.

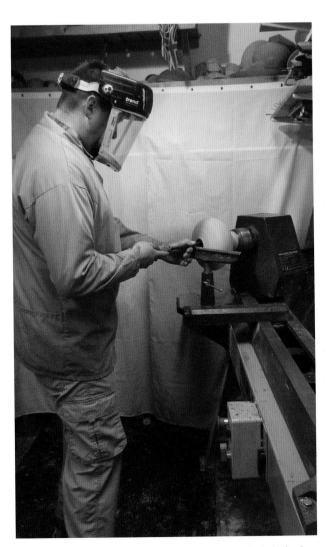

Good hollowing stance with no need to bend over the lathe bed.

Lathe configuration without good access for hollowing.

A swivel-head lathe allows safe access for hollowing.

A selection of drive and tail centers.

CHUCKS AND LATHE ACCESSORIES

Being able to hold and support the work safely while working is a must. There are various items available to help you to do that.

If you are working between centers with lumber that has the grain running parallel to the axis of the lathe bed, then a drive spur and a revolving center will help to shape the work initially. There are numerous ones to choose from; a ¾–1-in. (20–25mm) two- or four-prong drive spur will be ideal, and a standard revolving 60° point or revolving ring center will be fine. I favor a revolving ring center. It locates positively with the outer ring, spreading the load and preventing the point from penetrating the wood too far or splitting small sections. If you remove the wood and need to re-center it later, as with the friction drive chucking methods shown later, you will have a perfect ring mark to locate into.

The ring does not crush or deviate like a compressed cone-shaped hole. However, these cannot help you with the final shaping and hollowing; if you need to access the end of the work, you need to consider using a chuck to support the work while you do this.

I favor a scroll or geared chuck – a 4-in. (100mm) version is my preferred option for holding my work when hollowing. Most chucks come with a set of jaws that help you hold about 2¼–3¼ in. (55–81mm) in compression mode and from about 2⅜–3½ in. (60–90mm) in expansion mode – although I tend only to use tenons to hold my work. If you work on bigger projects than those featured in this book, you might need a larger set of jaws. All makes have various sizes for use on their chucks so you will have plenty of choice.

Scroll/geared chucks offer a solid and versatile work-holding solution.

Faceplates are available for both small and large projects.

If you are turning bowl/cross-grain forms – where the grain is running at 90° to the lathe bed – you will need to secure the blank to the lathe while you shape it. I typically use a screw chuck, as shown on the opposite page. This shows an attachment to fit in the chuck and is usually supplied with the chuck when bought. You can also buy dedicated screw chucks to fit directly on the spindle thread of the lathe.

If you choose to, you can initially mount both types of grain direction blanks on a faceplate, and this is the only mounting method you need. You will, however, need to account for the screws being inserted into the wood. These need to be long enough and fat enough to support the work fully when you turn. There will also be some waste wood with this method – more so than with a chuck. You need enough wood to work the shape

you require without turning anywhere near the screws in the bottom of the blank. Many successful hollow-form turners use this method, especially when working on larger projects.

To help with hollowing, especially when making the initial hole in the end of the blank prior to shaping the inside, it is helpful, and sometimes quicker, to first drill a hole in the piece that is just smaller than the required finished opening size and deep enough. A drill chuck with a selection of sawtooth or Forstner bits will help you do this. The drill chuck fits into the tailstock quill on the lathe (they come with 1, 2 or 3 Morse tapers to help you do this); once connected, they will accept various types of bits to help you drill the wood. The drill chuck can also be used in the headstock to hold polishing cloths or small pieces of wood and such like too, so it is a handy piece of equipment.

Sawtooth bits and Jacobs chucks offer an efficient method for drilling out forms prior to hollowing.

I often use a friction-drive method for refining and finishing the outside and bottom of vessels, bowls, platters and other items after the hollowing and internal shaping is complete. How the work is held between centers varies a little according to the specific project. The three methods shown below are quick, easy and low-cost ways to show you the principle and get you started with this process – you will find many ways of adapting these to suit your needs, so don't be afraid to experiment.

1 Typically you will use a configuration like this on bowls and forms with a wide opening. A waste section of wood is turned to have a domed face on the top. This domed face has been faced off with protective duct tape, non-slip router mat, or something that is not too thick and compresses easily, such as a couple of layers of paper towel. This is a protective covering that prevents the friction drive from marking your work. The curvature and size of the friction drive will vary from project to project. Keep all your waste sections of wood, as they will come in handy for this purpose.

2 The next stage is to place your work up against the friction drive; bring up the tailstock and center it on the center mark you have already marked from your earlier mounting method, and gently secure everything in place. If you mounted the piece between centers, there will be a center mark; if you do bowl work without the use of tailstock support, then it is worthwhile marking the center of what will be your recess or tenon so you can use this method later on.

This method leaves a small nub underneath the revolving center. If you use a point, the cone can split and this causes a major safety problem. If you use a ring center, this is less likely to happen, but don't make the cone too small – this is all you are holding the work in place with. After the refining and sanding is complete, remove the piece from the lathe, cut off the cone section left and blend in to the rest of the work as required.

3 If the wall thickness is not ultra-thin, you can use a variant of the previous technique to have a cone-shape friction drive locate into the opening of the vessel.

4 You can create stepped-shape cones of various sizes. Wood to wood might be a problem if the item slips during this process, as you will end up with a burnish mark or even a scorched ring if it goes wrong. But once you have the size of drive required, mount the work between centers as before.

5 There are times when the work is so fragile or thin-walled that supporting the work from the far end will place the work under too much load. It is better in this case to have a long section of wood that fits in the opening that is long enough to touch the very bottom of the inside of your work in line with the tailstock center.

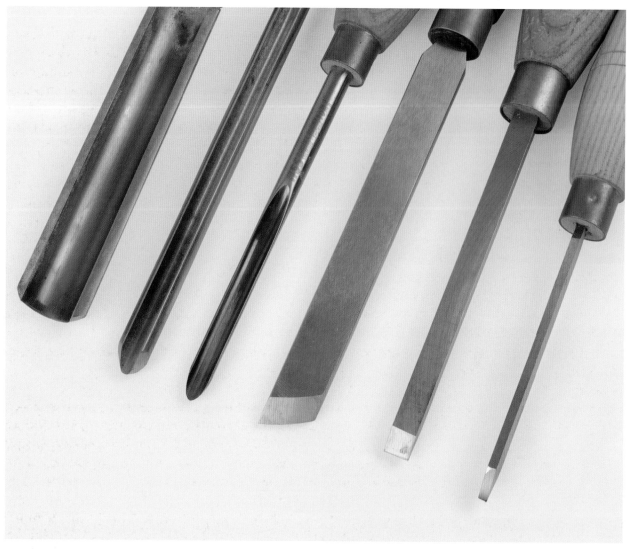

A basic selection of quality tools is often all that is needed.

BASIC TURNING TOOLS

I always try to keep things as simple as possible, and that includes the number of tools I use. There are so many to choose from that it can be quite confusing. This book assumes that you know how to use the basic tools already. My basic set includes the following:

- 1-in. (25mm) spindle roughing gouge – for the initial shaping of spindle work.
- ½-in. (12mm) bowl gouge – for the initial roughing and shaping of bowls and the outside of forms where a large overhang from the tool rest is required.
- ⅜-in. (10mm) bowl gouge – for refining the shape and finishing cuts on bowls and the outside of forms where a large overhang from the tool rest is required.

- ¼- or ⅜-in. (6 or 10mm) spindle gouge – for refining and fine detail on spindle work.
- 1-in. (25mm) and ½-in. (12mm) rolled-edge skew chisels – for refining detail and rolling beads on spindle work.
- ¼-in. (6mm) and ⅛-in. (3mm) parting tools – for parting cuts on both parallel-grain (spindle) and cross-grain (bowl) work.
- 1-in. (25mm) square-end scraper – for refining the surface finish on convex surfaces such as the outside of bowls and hollow forms.
- 1-in. (25mm) round-nose scraper for refining concave surfaces such as the inside of bowls or deep open vessels.
- ¼-in. (6mm) point tool to produce fine detailed grooves as a surface texture or for adding interest to the base of bowls and other forms.

HOLLOWING TOOLS

Hollowing tools come in various shapes and sizes to suit all types of work. I aim here to break down the common types available, look at how they are used, and what you need to consider when using them. It is worth noting that, although many come with handles, it is more common to buy them unhandled and fit them in an interchangeable handle that suits you.

HOOK AND RING TOOLS

Hook tools are some of the earliest turning tools you are likely to encounter and they are still commonly used by pole turners. They have a round main shaft with a tapered and flattened front taper that is bent to create a curve or curled head. The round shaft helps you easily manipulate the cutting edge of the tool. The cutting edge was typically on the leading edge, with a bevel in the inner edge of the tool. The outer face was rubbed against the work. This is also a bevel-rubbing tool. There could be two cutting edges – one on each side; this was not so common in older tools, but is more common in newer ones. Hook tools can be seen on the left-hand side of the picture below. Note that the outer two have an offset head. This is a common feature and helps with the presentation angle of the cutting edge to the work. Most modern hook tools have forged, cast or machined tips that fit into a shaft.

The modern variant of the hook tool is the ring tool, which can be seen in the three tools on the right in the picture below.

Typically comprising a ring attached to a straight main shaft, a more modern variant is a machined head attached to a shaft. Often with this type, the head position can be altered and locked in a new position to achieve a similar result to a cranked hook tool. Typically they have two cutting edges: one side of the ring has the bevel on the outside of the ring; the other has it on the inside. Both are used in the same way, and both also act as bevel-rubbing tools and have similar presentation angles to the work when cutting. It is worth remembering that no matter what cutting edge is offered against the work, the lower half of that edge should be doing the cutting, never the upper section.

These tools are more commonly used on wet end-grain work, but can be used on dry work, too. Proficient users of this tool can use them on bowl work, too – again, damp or wet wood is more commonly employed when using them. I like to use them on forms with a wider opening at the top. The typically available shapes of this type of tool do not lend themselves to working on tight shoulders and undercuts.

Although hook and ring tools are still made and regularly used in mainland Europe, they are not so common in the UK and the rest of the world. That is a shame, as they are true cutting tools, and once you have learnt how to use them they are a delight to work with.

From left to right: the historical transition from hook, to ring to shielded hollowing tools.

USING A HOOK TOOL

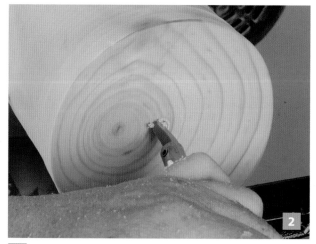

1 This tool has two cutting edges: one on the left and one on the right. When turning on the inside of work, the tool should cut on or just above center. For this cutting sequence we will use an end-grain piece of wood. We will have to cut from the center out toward the outer edge of the work to ensure we cut with the grain.

2 There is a need to create a central hole in the work so the tool can start a cut. You can bore a hole for this, or reverse the tool so that the right-hand side of the cutter in the previous picture is rotated left and what is the top open section of the tool points downward. With the cutting edge set to about the 10 o'clock position if viewed as a clock face, or about 45° to the left of vertical, and the edge just to the right of center, enter into the wood, pulling the tool into the center section. The tool will cut and you need to stop just after the cutting edge has passed the center point.

3 Now rotate the tool toward the right so the other cutting edge can be used and the opening of the cutting edge is uppermost. The cutting edge should point to about 10 o'clock. If the tool cutting edge is horizontal to the work, the whole cutting edge technically could be made to cut the wood. Controlling the depth of cut is problematic; what typically happens is the cutting edge is dragged into the wood and a catch ensues. By presenting the edge to the work so it creates a slicing cut you end up being able to control and limit the amount of edge in contact with the work. When the cutting edge is horizontal to the work, the cut is fierce and aggressive; when the edge is rotated toward the 45° or 10 o'clock position, it is more refined and gentle; if the cutting edge is nearer the vertical, it makes the most refined and gentle cuts of all.

4 Once you have the cut, arc or pull the cutting edge out toward the outer edge. You can either glide the tool along the tool rest or arc from the center out, using the intersection of the tool shaft and tool rest as a pivot point to produce your required shape. While you have waste wood available, you can play with presenting the tool edge at various angles to see what happens. Keep the lathe speed low, at around 600 rpm, to diminish the chances of a major mishap if you get a catch. Pine and sycamore void of knots or inclusions are excellent practice woods to get the hang of this tool.

5 Extend the cut to the required position.

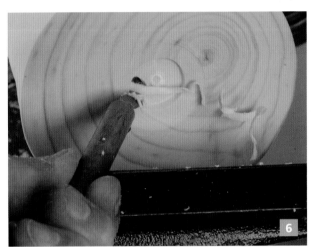

6 You can see the type of shaving a slicing cut produces on this damp wood.

7 Make successive cuts, deepening as with the first cuts shown, followed by the opening shaping cuts as needed.

HANDY HINT

Maintaining a sharp cutting edge is essential on any tool, so my mantra is "sharpen little and often," according to the manufacturer's instructions. If a tool is presented to the wood correctly, the forces induced are transferred down the shaft into the tool rest, making for an efficient cut. However, if you find you are struggling to hold onto a tool or are unable to control the cut, stop and check the tool presentation. Use the pictures in this chapter to see what you are doing differently and alter accordingly. You will always feel when a tool is cutting efficiently as it will glide through the wood. Never struggle with a tool; this will eventually lead to an accident.

1 We will start with the cutting edge of the side with the bevel on the inside of the ring. Use the same presentation used with the first cut for the hook tool on page 50.

2 Using the lower half of the cutting edge and the open face of the ring pointing at the 10 o'clock position, enter into the wood to remove the central nub. The cutting edge enters into the wood just past the center.

3 Once you have the central hole, rotate the ring so that you use the edge where the bevel is on the outside of the ring.

4 Using the same cutting angle, gradually arc out from the center toward the outer edge or required position. You can see the long peeling cut achieved and the cut occurring in the lower half of the cutting edge. Repeat the sequence of cuts as before to achieve the required depth and shape.

A small selection of fixed-head hollowing tools.

FIXED-HEAD HOLLOWING TOOLS

This is a general term applied to tools that have a cutting edge fixed in one position to the shaft on which it fits. Some have interchangeable or replaceable tips; others have a solid bar that has a cutting edge ground on the bar itself. There are a few variants; for example, some fixed-head tools have a tip that can be moved from a scrape to a shear cut.

The types of shaft include round-bar; square-section; round-bar with flats on; and rectangular-section. All are designed to hold a cutter or cutting edge of some sort. Some of the tool shafts are straight; others have a curve in them so you can reach into the shoulders of curved forms. Some tools are designed to allow you to present the cutter in one presentation angle only – typically the swan-necked tools or the square- and rectangular-shafted tools. Others allow you to rotate a blade to move the cutter from a horizontal scraping-type cut to one that peels the wood.

The round-bar ones offer the most versatility, depending on the shape of the shank – you cannot move swan-necked tools through many presentation positions. However, tools with a round-bar section allow the cutter to be presented to the surface of the wood at various angles depending upon the cut required. The more the shaft is rotated counter-clockwise, the more the cutting edge approaches a shear angle, reducing the forces on the cutting edge and tool. If a more aggressive cut is required, then simply rotate the tool back clockwise until the cutter is horizontal. This takes more practice to control than using a tool with a square section shaft or one with a flat resting section; however, these in turn can limit the versatility of the tool.

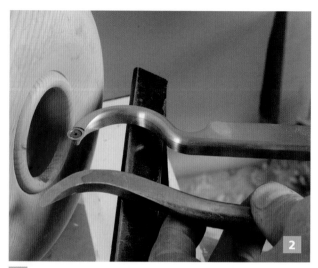

1 When deciding what tool you require, you need to know the opening size you are working through and the shape of the item you are to make. It could be that a straight tool will do everything you need. Here we have a gentle-shouldered hollow form with quite a large opening. The ruler shows the central line of the tool. Note that the side of the shaft is touching the side of the opening, which means a straight tool will not quite work for this shape. A swan-necked tool, or even a straight one with a swivel tip – as shown in the next section, on page 56 – could be used in this instance.

2 For hollow forms with a large undercut shoulder, you need a tool that will reach under that shoulder easily; a tool with a curve or swan-neck shape will help you do this.

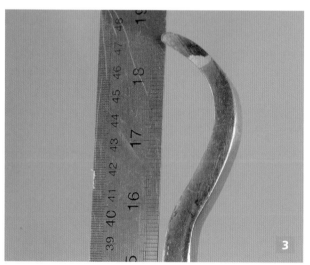

3 Swan-necked, articulated or crank-necked tools have the cutting tips designed to be in line with the main straight shaft section of the tool.

4 Never have any part of the offset or curve on the tool rest. If you do this, you shift the control point from the straight section so that it is in line with the part touching the rest. This makes the tool hard to control and the blade is liable to twist during the cut.

5 The longer the overhang of the tool past the tool rest – the fulcrum point – the more leverage you need to counter it. This can be done by increasing the length of the tool, which might include a handle of some sort behind the rest. You could also increase the weight of the section behind the rest or combine both methods to maintain control.

6 The deeper you go into the work, or the further the blade is over the rest, the thicker the diameter of shaft you will need to counter the flexing in the blade that overhangs the rest. Using a bigger-shanked tool means working through a larger hole. Typically, a ¼-in. (6mm)-diameter shank on the tool will enable you to go to a maximum of about 3 in. (75mm) before you encounter excessive flexing in the blade. A ½-in. (12mm) shank will reach about 6–7 in. (150–175mm) maximum before encountering excessive flexing – subject to the presentation angle of the tip; how much cutter is in contact with the wood; and the nature of the wood being cut.

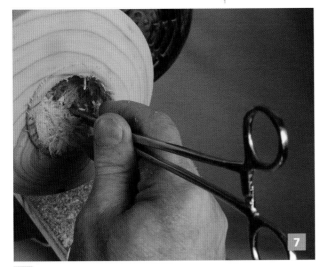

7 When working on the inside of hollow forms, the shavings gather at the widest part of the interior. The shape and size of the cuttings vary according to the type of tool and how wet or dry the lumber is. If these shavings are not removed regularly, the build-up will prevent the tip from cutting.

HANDY HINTS

The downside with not having any part of the offset or curve on the rest is that it places an overhang of the cutting edge past the rest. If this overhang is too great in relation to the shaft size, it will induce vibration, and the blade will flex and chatter.

Never place your fingers in the spinning work to remove the debris. Instead, stop the lathe and use whatever tool or item you can to best reach in safely to remove the debris. Forceps are excellent for this, but bent wire, wood, a spoon or something similar would also work. Do not remove the piece from the chuck as you are unlikely to get everything recentralized when putting it back. If you have to, remove the piece while it is still attached to the chuck or faceplate in order to remove the debris; it should then be easy to relocate it and carry on.

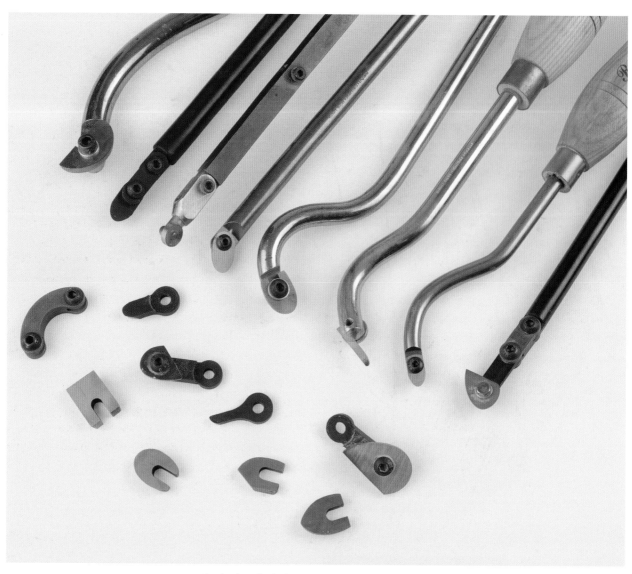

A selection of swivel and articulated hollowing tools.

SWIVEL AND ARTICULATED HOLLOWING TOOLS

The main difference between these and the fixed-tip tools is that the tips can be moved to a new cutting position or interchanged with tips with other shapes, usually by means of a machine screw attachment. In some cases, the shanks of the tool may not be a fixed shape; some feature a knuckle- or link-type section that changes the tool from a straight shank to one that is articulated.

This allows you to change the shape to reach under sharp curved sections, for example; in most cases you can also alter the tip position. Many manufacturers supply a range of different cutter tips for such tools.

These tools are used in the same way as the fixed-tip tools, but here are some tips that will help you get the most from them.

> **HANDY HINT**
> With any hollowing tool, it is vital that the
> articulation projects beyond the tool rest, with the
> tool being supported by the straight section of the shaft
> to give maximum support and control.

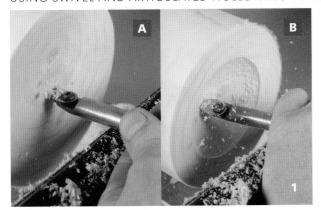

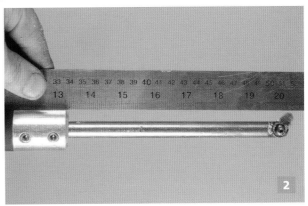

1 With any style of hollowing tool, the type, shape and size of cutting edge and its presentation to the work affects the amount of downward pressure exerted on the cutting tip. Typically, a scraping tip presented horizontally to the work **A** will encounter more downward pressure than the same tip presented at a shear cutting angle of 45° **B** . This also applies to how much cutting edge is in contact with the wood at any one time. The more there is in contact, the greater the pressures involved.

2 With swivelling tips and articulated sections, make sure that the cutting tip is, as close as possible, in line with the shaft of the tool. Any offset will increase the downward pressure. Since the tool's control point is the shank of the tool in contact with the tool rest, you want to minimize this downward pressure as much as possible.

3 When working at any depth in a hollow form, you are likely to lose sight of the tip of the tool. It is important that you know what is happening inside and also where you are cutting – or you can end up with a catch.

4 A simple technique is to mark the shaft of the blade. Alternatively, if you use an interchangeable handle, use the screws in the handle so that when the mark or the screws are vertical your tool tip is horizontal.

5 This will give you a quick and easy indicator without stooping down and trying to see what is happening inside.

A selection of shielded-cutter hollowing tools.

SHIELDED-CUTTER TOOLS

Shielded cutters are modern-day reworkings of the hook and ring tools featured earlier (see pages 49–52). These are true cutting tools, not scraping tools. They typically have a ring or hook cutting tip, over which is placed a guard or shield. The cutting tip can be moved in relation to the shield to expose specific parts of the cutting edge to help you cut efficiently on various parts of a hollow form. The shield is effectively a cut limiter. As with a hook or ring tool, the shavings are usually ejected from underneath the cutter, although a few eject the shavings from the top of the shield.

It is important to note that these tools are not bevel-rubbing tools. That is the major difference between these and the hook and ring tools, although even these can be used with no bevel rub to create a scraping action.

The tools may have a fixed-shape shaft – straight or swan-necked – or have articulated links on the shaft. Some come with a moveable tip and others with a fixed tip. Whatever type you use it is worth noting that this type of cutter – as with the ring and hook tools – creates bigger shavings than scraping tips do, so you may need to stop more often to clear out the debris that gathers inside forms.

HANDY HINT

When selecting a shielded hollowing tool, consider the application for which it is to be used. Some tools are designed to suit open forms where access is not restricted. But if you prefer to turn hollow forms where cutting is achieved through a much smaller opening, the size and versatility of the articulation will be a major consideration. If in doubt, try before you buy.

1 Here is a typical shielded cutter with an articulated shaft section set so the shaft is straight.

2 When the shield or guard is adjusted correctly you will be able to present this type of tip horizontally to the wood (something you cannot do with a ring or hook tool) without the risk of a bite or catch. Note how the cutter is exposed all the way around the cutting edge. You can limit what part of the edge shows.

3 The cutter, as with the other tools shown so far, should cut on or just above center when working on the inside of any work, preferably with a very slight trailing action to lessen the downward pressures. You start by creating a small central hole with the tip of the tool, or by drilling a hole first.

HANDY HINTS

The forces associated when hollowing with the overhang from the tool rest to the cutting tip can be controlled to some extent by what I refer to as "shaping the cut." This is achieved by the presentation of the cutting edge in relation to the wood that alters the forces exerted on it.

If you find controlling the tool becomes problematic the deeper you go, simply rotate the shaft counter-clockwise by 10–20 degrees; this will present the cutter in a trailing mode, in turn lessening the twisting forces exerted upon it. Likewise, the cutting edge can be rotated clockwise back to the horizontal if a more aggressive cut is required.

Rotating counter-clockwise is a technique I frequently use when hollowing deep without being able to view the cutting tip. The cut is gently picked up with the shaft being rotated clockwise until a controllable cut is achieved.

4 You then sweep the cutter outward to create the desired shape. To rough out the work, you can push and pull as required. However, cutting with the grain – in this case cutting from the center out toward the edge – will give a better surface finish to the two cuts.

5 These tools allow you to rotate the edge so you can shear the wood to create an even better surface finish.

HANDY HINTS
When cutting with a hollowing tool, maximize the intersection of the tool shaft and tool rest to produce a fulcrum from which to work. Cutting in arcs from this fulcrum will produce smooth curves in the base of the form as well as facilitating an efficient cutting action, especially when the view into the vessel is restricted.

6 Unlike the tool shown in steps 4 and 5, where the shavings exited underneath the shield, with this tool the shavings exit from the top of the shield.

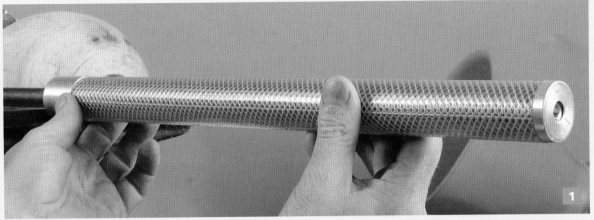

1 Always be aware of where you are cutting. An aspect of hollowing that people might not be aware of or forget about is that cutting on the inside of a hollow form or even a box or bowl should occur on or above center. When working at depth it is easy to lose sight of not only the tip of the tool and its position but also where the tip is cutting in relation to the center height.

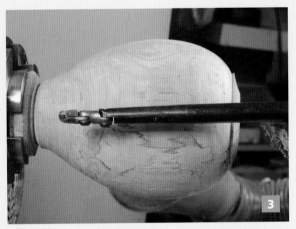

2 Presenting the tool shaft to slightly trail helps to produce a stable cut with any of the hollowing tools. When using scrapers this is a must, as with standard presentation of these tools. Even a slight trailing shaft will be magnified the farther the tool reaches from the tool rest.

3 Taking this trailing into account, the tool rest should be raised the deeper you hollow to avoid cutting below center. This trailing angle is a very natural cutting position in producing a stable cut.

HANDY HINT

A problem can arise when hollowing into a deep form: the raising of the tool rest too high can cause the top of the tool shaft to touch the top opening during hollowing. This should be avoided. Lowering your body stance by bending slightly at the knees can reduce the amount of trail, raising the cutting tip and thus reducing the need to excessively raise the tool rest.

HOLLOWING RIGS

The projects in this book deal with the basics of creating hollow forms. The projects are completed using hand tools with freestyle hand turning with no additional supports per se. That said, you will encounter downward pressure on the tool during hollowing and this, coupled with a long reach of the tool over the rest, may present problems with regard to controlling the tool and thereby the cut.

There are hollowing rigs and systems available that act as stabilizers and prevent the lifting of the rear end of a tool caused by the downward pressure. Many turners who regularly turn mid- or large-sized hollow forms use this type of unit. They aid the process by reducing the physicality of the turning process so you can concentrate on the shaping and turning. If you decide you like creating such forms, this is something you could look into. There are many variants, but here we feature three to show how they are typically set up.

One of the many types of hollowing rig in use.

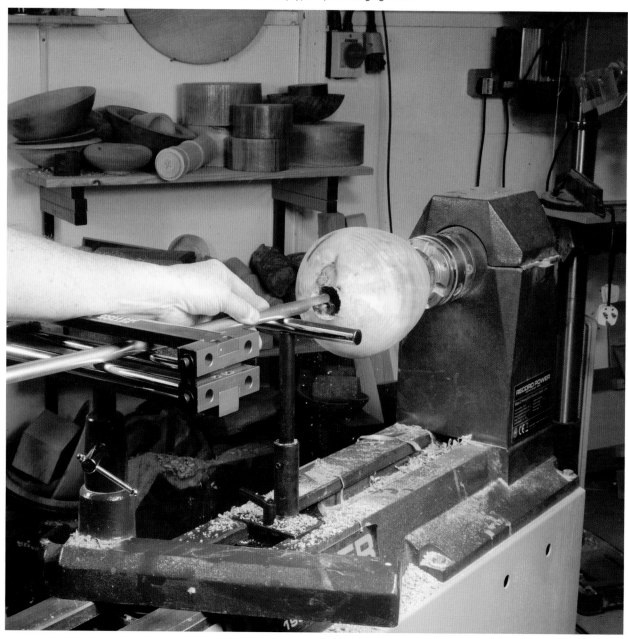

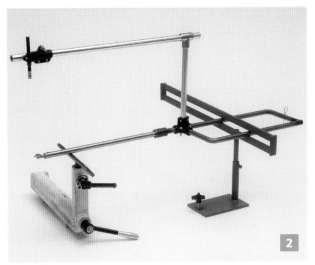

1 For this version there is a handle into which a hollowing tool can be fitted – a swivel-tipped tool is supplied with this kit. The shaft has a flat underside so the tool cannot rotate during the cut. The shaft is designed to fit through a wide horizontal parallel roller bar adjustable "gate." The top bar of this must sit very close to the top of the bar and prevent the tool from rotating while still allowing it to move through the bars.

The front section of the tool sits on the tool rest and the gate system is adjusted to match the rest height so that the tool can cut on or just above center height. The gate system is locked on the lathe bed, but is adjustable so you can set it where you need it to go. The shaft of the tool glides through the parallel roller bars. Because everything is held in a given plane and stabilized with no lifting, you just maneuver the tool sideways or backward and forward, with the tool shaft always on the rest so you can cut the required shape.

2 A variant of the first rig is one where there is a tubular D-section rear handle arrangement – or a rectangular bar section – that fits in a gate similar to the one mentioned above. This type of system does not need to have a tool shaft with a flat on it to prevent rotation during the cut because the D-shaped handle arrangement is always in the support gate. You can fit many types of hollowing tool in this system. Again, the tool shaft sits on the tool rest. Many of the rigs can be fitted with laser pointing devices; once set up in relation to the cutting tip, these can be set up to indicate wall thickness as you turn, thus saving a lot of time stopping and measuring.

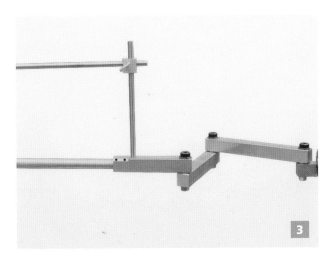

3 Another variation has no "gates" to speak of but an articulated elbow arrangement instead. The rear end locks onto the tailstock quill or has a Morse taper that fits in the quill. The front end of the elbow arrangement of links accepts a hollowing tool, which, once again, is supported at the cutting end on the normal tool rest. Since the system is absolutely in line with the center of the lathe spindle, the tool will cut on or very slightly above center. The articulated links easily allow you to move the tool as required.

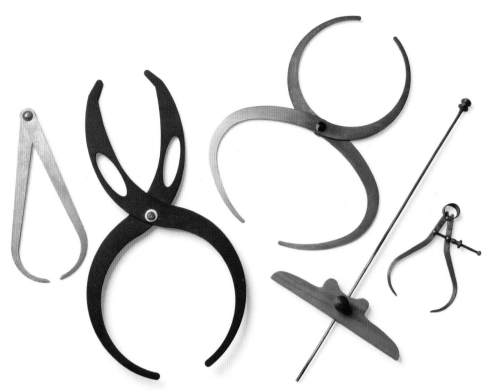

A selection of callipers and depth gauges, which form an important part of a turner's equipment.

MEASURING AND MARKING

I try to keep things simple at all times. It is vital that you always know what is happening, and that includes the wall thickness. I typically use a double-ended figure-of-eight shaped pair of callipers that allows me to get inside most of the hollow forms I make. There are numerous types of callipers to choose from, giving you plenty of options to suit the shapes you will make.

I use a depth gauge in addition to the callipers. This is a homemade affair that has a cross-beam of wood through the center of which a piece of ¼-in. (6mm) dowel is passed. The hole drilled is a tight fit so you can adjust the dowel to the depth required; the cross-beam sits on top of the work so you have an accurate reference point. Alternatively, you can have a threaded screw to lock a section of wire or dowel at a given point.

> **HANDY HINT**
> Always check your measurements twice before you start cutting to avoid mistakes, as you can always remove more wood but you cannot replace it if you cut too deeply and ultimately through the side of the form.

ABRASIVES

Sanding is a generic term that covers the use of abrasives to refine the surface of the work. There are numerous types of abrasive and it can sometimes be baffling as to what type to use. A good flexible-backed aluminium-oxide abrasive in grit grades from 100 down to 400 is likely to serve you well when sanding wood. When using coarse-grit grades, have the lathe speed set low so you allow the abrasive to cut. The first grade used must remove any surface damage. Don't skip grades thereafter. If you start at 100 grit, then go to 120 grit, 180 grit, and so on.

Each grade used after the previous one is designed only to remove the scratches left from the previous one used. Finer-grit grades are available if you need them. Abrasives can be used for hand or power sanding. The arbors are shown on the left-hand side, top of page 65. Many of you will already be familiar with these, and many of you will use these for power sanding. Designed to fit in a drill, they hold an abrasive via a hook-shaped facing. This requires any abrasive to be used with them to have a fabric-loop backing so that is held on the hook facing on the arbor.

A selection of arbors and abrasives available to the turner.

SANDING ACCESSORIES

Power sanding is a fast and easy way to sand work but, given the types of hollow forms you are likely to create, power sanders will not easily reach any distance into your work when held on a drill and will certainly not work on undercut surfaces. Therefore, you need to look at other options to reach in the work; you do not want to stick your fingers too far in the work, and certainly not your hand and arm, even if you could. Below are a few store-bought options. Some, as with the one on the left, are designed to hold a sanding arbor in the chuck end; the other end is placed in the drill. The central core of this rotates by means of bearings,

but the outer section, which you hold, does not. This allows you to sand at depth, as long as you can fit the shaft of the tool in the opening hole and, of course, as long as the shape is relatively easy to reach.

The two tools on the far right have a hook-face ball onto which you place abrasives. These are held in the hand, or placed in an interchangeable handle. They do not rotate, but are manipulated against the inside of work – a variant of hand sanding with a block holding the abrasive.

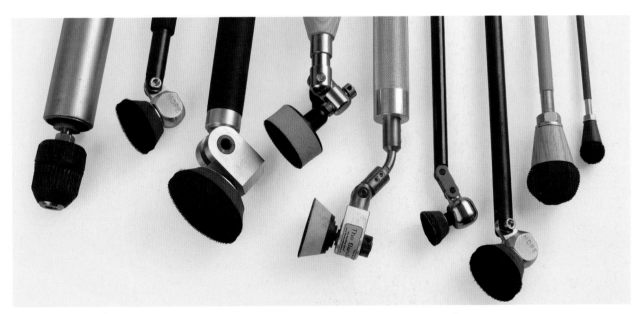

Inertia and fixed-head sanding arbors.

Fixed-head sanding arbor being used inside a form; the handle is trailing slightly, with the head being presented to center height of the form.

SANDING UNDERCUTS

You will need another method to sand undercuts. The other units shown in the picture are articulated self-powered heads. Utilizing normal power-sanding arbors that are placed in bearings, these tools will rotate freely when offered up to the work with the lower edge of the arbor in contact with it, allowing you to sand a surface easily. Make sure that the arbor and the shaft of the tool used fit in the opening – there are various options available for you to do this.

The undercut to be finished can dictate if a fixed head or articulated arbor is to be used.

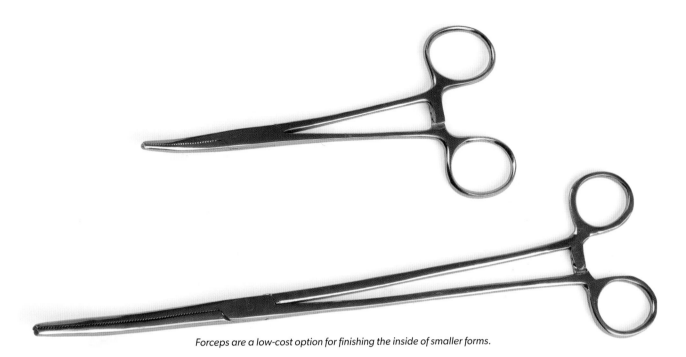

Forceps are a low-cost option for finishing the inside of smaller forms.

There are, of course, homemade options, too. Forceps can be used to hold an abrasive by wrapping it around the curved tip section (you can get straight versions, too, and both types come in various lengths); this allows you to sand internal and external curves with ease. This tool makes it easy to clean out shavings, and can also be used for sanding.

Never place your fingers in the holes of the forceps; hold them on the outside. If you have your fingers in the holes and get a catch in the hollow form you may get dragged round with the forceps and snap your fingers.

You could also consider removing a cutting tip from one of your hollowing tools and wrapping abrasives around the end of the shank – this is a low-cost option.

Forceps being used with good support over the tool rest into the form.

FINISHES

It is vital to pick the right finish for the task in hand and to create the required effect. For a utility bowl turned to hold foodstuffs, a food-safe oil finish will be required. If a soft tactile sheen is important, a Danish or similar oil would be suitable. If the piece is purely aesthetic, then a buffed wax or spray finish may be more suitable since the piece will not be handled frequently. These and many other factors affect your choice of finish.

Finishes can be broken down into three main categories:

OILS

You can apply oils straight to the freshly finished surface. I like to use them because they are easy to apply, often giving a deep soft sheen to the wood. Oil finishes can, however, darken the wood so this is worth considering prior to choosing the best option for your project.

WAXES

A wax should be applied to the wood after it has been sealed with an appropriate sanding sealer. It can then be buffed either on or off the lathe.

SPRAY FINISHES

Another option is to use spray finishes, which often come in aerosol cans for spraying a fine topcoat onto the project once sealed with an appropriate sanding sealer. Types available include cellulose, acrylic and melamine. They give a hard-wearing surface but without care can sit on the surface, giving a rather plastic effect.

SAMPLE BOARD

Whatever type you choose, create a sample board from the wood you are using for your project so you can try out different finishes on it. I typically use oils, because they are easy to use and can accept finishes such as wax over them if required. I also use spray lacquer – again, they are easy to apply and you can buy them to create any luster. Lacquers do not darken the wood as much as oils, but are a film finish that is less tactile. I often use wax as a top finish, but again, the choice is yours.

> ### HANDY HINT
> Always purchase the best-quality finish you can afford; the finish is the icing on the cake, and cheap variants can often leave less than desirable results.

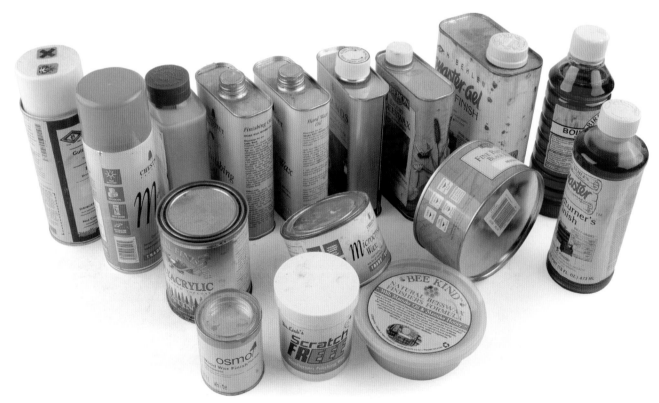

A small selection of finishes available to the turner.

BUFFING

The term *buffing* is often used in conjunction with using a handheld pad, brush or, more commonly, for turners having a wheel comprising fabric that is loaded or contains some abrasive material in order to refine a surface – often after a finish is supplied, although bare materials such as metal, wood and plastics can be buffed too.

I typically use a lathe-mounted buffing wheel loaded with micro-fine abrasive. Many types are available in different grit grades down to those measured in microns. While this is held securely on the lathe and spinning at an appropriate speed, I manipulate my finished work against it to improve the surface finish.

There are many types of buffing wheels. Some are quite hard and best used with coarse abrasives and on such materials as metals. Others are softer and better for refinishing surfaces with finer grit grades. The finest grades of abrasive and softer wheels are best used to finish off surface finishes and plastics. You can go so fine with the abrasives as to end up with a mirror finish on some materials with no scratches visible to the naked eye. You also have the option of loading finishing wax on a soft wheel so you can buff work evenly.

Buffing wheel, with the form presented to the lower section of the wheel.

Always keep the work moving and make sure you use the lower section of the wheel if it rotates toward you. Never offer a leading edge to the oncoming work; always have edges pointing downward and away from oncoming wheels. Remember to use a face shield and dust mask, too.

Selection of buffing pads for finishing both the inside and outside of forms.

CHAPTER FOUR

FORM

Form and shape are to some degree a subjective maze; one person's preference of a classic form might differ from another's modern take for the same project. However, by having an understanding of the foundation principles of how to construct, we are better prepared at the lathe when producing our projects. The more you view form the more you will see; it is an enjoyable subject that we can easily research in our local environment.

ANATOMY OF FORMS

In this chapter we will look at form and how it is constructed, taking into account proportions and other considerations. Many books have been published solely on the subject of design, shape and form, and the subject may seem daunting initially. However, having some basic knowledge will better prepare you at the lathe for getting the most from your projects. As your knowledge expands you will be able to explore ideas armed with the understanding of what might work best.

RESEARCHING AND OBSERVING FORM

Woodturning is a never-ending journey. Once you have grasped the information in this chapter, you may wish to engage in further research.

The Internet and library are useful resources on the subject; the more we stimulate our minds with research, the more natural the process of turning a good form becomes. Do not restrict your learning only to forms within woodturning; most forms originally came from ancient pottery and ceramics, while other valuable sources of inspiration include forms within glasswork and patterns within textiles.

Any object around us has the potential to teach us about form. For example, the building in 1 and the fruit in 2 contain shapes and forms that could be incorporated into a project.

The main roof of the building, if turned upside down, could be used to produce the main form for a bowl or vase. The fruit in itself is a perfect form that could be used for a hollow form or a vase.

Keeping a camera or a sketchpad with you is a useful way to build up a reference library of shapes and ideas for your work. Visit museums and places of interest or go for a walk to study the shapes and forms in your local environment. Take a photo or sketch items that you find inspiring so you can use them later. Once you hone your observation skills, you will find that shape, form and design can be found all around you, and these can be used to aid the development of ideas.

ANATOMY OF FORM

Before looking at how to construct a form, it is important to understand the anatomy and labels given to the individual parts within a turned form.

Form is the word given to the shape, visual appearance or make-up of an object as a whole. It is not limited to solid objects, but for the purpose of this book we will concern ourselves only with the solid form.

Objects are made up of separate parts or shapes that, when added together, make the form. As an example, see **3**, a 2D drawing showing the outline or shape of a form. In this example you will see the separate parts and the names given to each. A 2D drawing is made up of a line or lines that visually describe the individual geometric shapes. Added together, these give a 2D representation of the form but not the form itself. The form is produced only when these 2D shapes are turned into the solid.

When starting turning, we generally produce shallow bowls and platters. From a technical point of view, these are considered a good place to start due to the ease of access for removing material from inside the vessel. As we progress, there is a desire to tackle more challenging forms. We will now look in detail at the different types of forms so we can understand their construction.

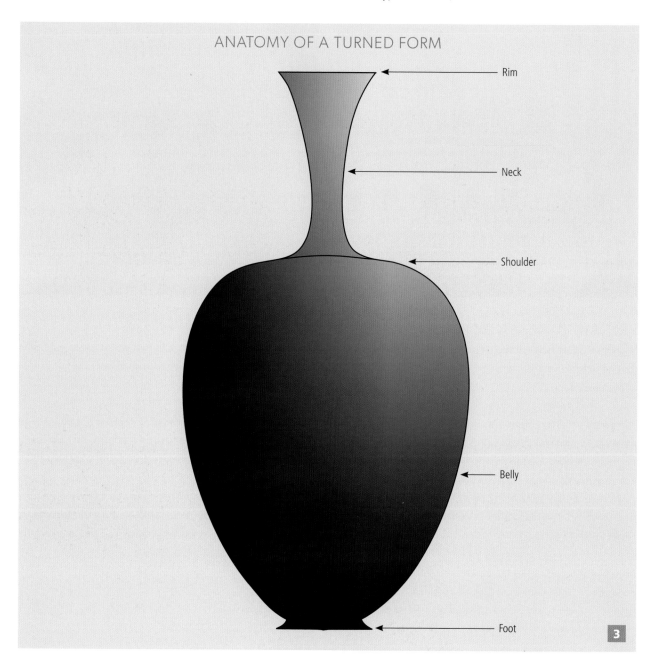

ANATOMY OF A TURNED FORM

— Rim

— Neck

— Shoulder

← Belly

← Foot

3

OPEN FORMS

An open form is one in which the flow of line to the rim continues outward and away from the central axis of the form, as in . Here the shape of the bowl is made up of a foot with the belly continuing to gradually curve away from the base and centerline, and the line continuing in an outward flow.

This form lends itself, but is not restricted, to utility items such as the rice or fruit bowl, where the storage and removal of produce is the main consideration. It is a simple yet beautiful form and often not as easy to turn with a flowing line as you might initially assume.

ENCLOSED FORMS

An enclosed form is one in which the main form or line flows back in toward the central axis of the form, as in . Examples of this include, but are not restricted to, vases and deep bowls.

HOLLOW FORMS

A hollow form is simply a progression of the enclosed form. The flow of the line continues from the shoulder inward toward the central axis of the form, with only a small hole remaining for tool access in which the cutting process cannot be viewed. An example is shown in . This type of form is often regarded as the most difficult to accomplish as it requires the maker to "feel" their way while removing material from the inside.

Although there are technical difficulties involved in producing hollow forms, I believe that most woodturners can start turning hollow forms early on in their career as long as they understand the process, know how to use the tools required, and practice enough. However, no matter how skilled we are with the tools, if we produce poor forms then technical prowess is of little relevance. A viewer of our work, besides other woodturners, will seldom be interested in the technical ability required to achieve the end result. Although I always advocate the use of good technique, a potential buyer (if you choose to sell your work) will decide in the first few seconds of viewing whether they find a form pleasing or not.

Open form

Enclosed form

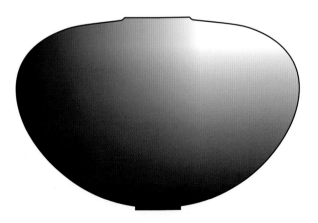

Hollow form

PROPORTION AND LINE

Now we have looked at the basic anatomy of form, we need to understand how to construct the separate shapes that go into a form while taking into account proportion and line.

Proportion is the correct relationship between the connecting parts of a form or an object. This subject is too vast to be fully covered in this book, although the amount of theory needed to produce a balanced form is relatively small. Achieving balance and harmony in a form is our aim; this is done through the use of correct proportion, both within the form as a whole and within the separate parts that make up the whole.

The *divine proportion,* also known as the *golden section* or the *golden ratio,* constructs proportion using a specific formula. Represented by the Greek letter phi, the value of the golden ratio is 1.618. This phenomenon has been studied for thousands of years and is commonly used within architecture, mathematics and art. It is not always simple to apply in the workshop without calculation, but is worth further study.

A simple and practical method for the application of proportion within design is the rule of thirds. Due to the ease of visualization, this is my preferred method of applying proportion within my own work. The rule of thirds, while differing from the divine proportion, produces similar results.

THE RULE OF THIRDS

The rule of thirds (which I will now refer to simply as the "rule"), allows us to add balance and proportion to a form, be it open, enclosed or hollow. It is a simple method used to structure the separate parts quickly with a ruler, pencil and simple mental arithmetic. After a little practice you will be able to apply the rule by eye alone.

7 shows a form illustrated with the thirds being marked to identify the relationship between the separate parts that make up the whole vase.

You will see in **8** that the rule is used for proportioning the main body and neck of the vase. This adds a relationship and harmony in relation to the separate parts – in this case, the body and neck – as well as connecting them together to give proportion to the piece as a whole. This is seen in the foot, belly, shoulder and neck. The parts have been divided into thirds in both height and width. The neck leading to the rim is also divided into thirds through its height and width.

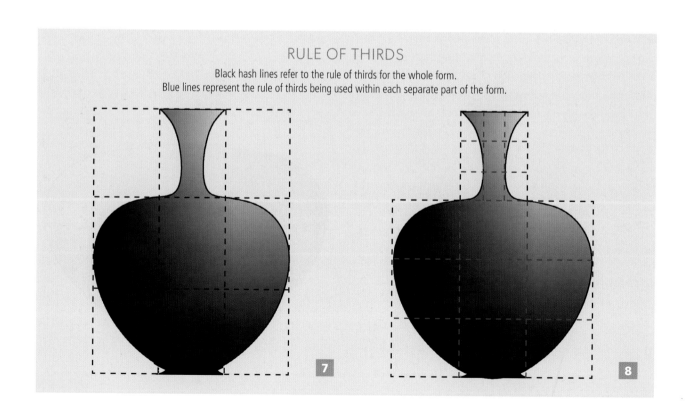

RULE OF THIRDS
Black hash lines refer to the rule of thirds for the whole form.
Blue lines represent the rule of thirds being used within each separate part of the form.

7

8

To work out the height for the upper section (in this instance the neck and rim) to comply with the rule, we simply produce the top to be half the height of the main body. Thus, when added, the top will be one-third the height of the piece as a whole.

A second example where the rule can be seen is in **9**, where the neck has been replaced with a lid and finial.

By taking the time to look closely at the proportions of objects around us we can understand why we might find a form appealing. Has the rule been applied? If so, where and how? By understanding how form is constructed we will be better placed to progress with our own designs and ideas.

The divisions within the rule will vary depending upon the type of project produced. A form designed for utility will have different requirements from that of a purely aesthetic form, and this will dictate how the rule is applied. An example of this would be a vase designed for displaying tall grasses; here the main consideration would be that of stability, with the aesthetics of form coming second. When applying the rule in this instance, the foot could be turned to be larger in diameter to satisfy the need for stability, as shown in **10**, while maintaining the rule vertically for the belly and shoulder. A similar design made purely for aesthetic appeal could include a foot of only one-third of the largest diameter, as stability beyond that of being displayed is not the main consideration – as previously shown in **9**.

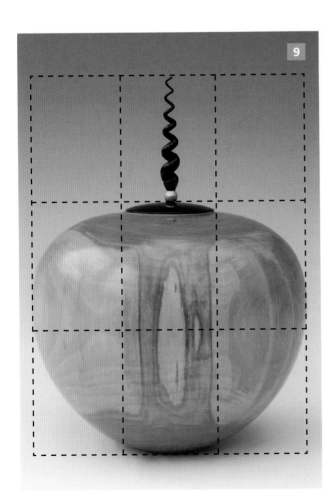

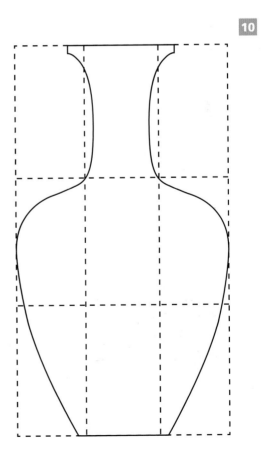

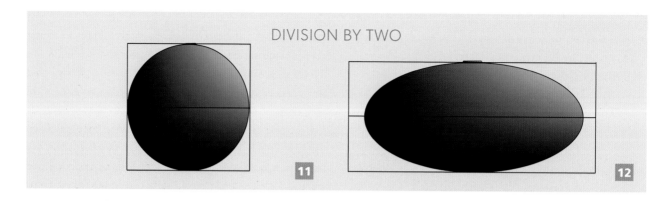

DIVISION BY TWO

11

12

Another method of proportion is that of division by two. This can give a less than satisfactory result of proportion unless used carefully for the height of certain aspects in a form. Examples of this are the join of a box or hollow form where the flow of line within each half is similar if not the same as the adjoining line. In this book this method works as an example within the sphere, **11**, or squashed sphere, **12**. In both, the measurement from the base to the shoulder is half the height of the form, with the flow of line both above and below being mirrored.

Although this method can be used when proportioning height and produces a pleasing form if treated with care, it is not a method of proportion that is adopted widely, in part due to its bland symmetry. I have limited it to the few examples here as an option. While this form looks simple in line it is not so simple to achieve on the lathe, as any change in line becomes obvious.

BREAKING THE RULES

You should be mindful that any "rule" is simply an aid in our work and not the be-all and end-all. We should not become slaves to any rule or we may inadvertently restrict the shapes we produce. My advice is that if you decide to break the rule, it should be obvious. An example of this is in **13**. Here you will see a representation of one of my favored forms. The flow of the

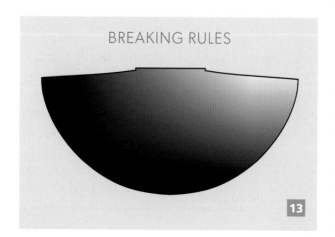

BREAKING RULES

13

RESEARCHING THE RULE
Spend ten minutes looking through an interiors magazine or at objects around your home. How many examples of the rule can you see? Don't look only at objects within the magazine; look at how the graphics and the text have been laid out. How has your table lamp been designed? Soon you will be looking at the objects you view in a different way, noticing where the rule has been applied or not.

line from the shoulder to the rim is very small in height and not in anyway related to the rule, which, having been broken so obviously in its height, gives a natural balance to the form.

Form, shape and color are to a certain degree subjective. However, there is a difference between deciding not to adhere to a rule and producing an unsatisfactory design without understanding why. With this brief explanation of form and proportion you will have a place from which to start and will be able to take this knowledge to the lathe.

FLOW OF LINE

If we view the silhouette of a wooden form, all we see is the shape void of depth, color or grain. The shape or line of a form is the most important factor to consider above and beyond the beauty of the wood. A beautiful form will enhance a bland piece of wood, but a beautiful piece of wood will not enhance a poor form.

To achieve a pleasing form, the lines are best when flowing smoothly; any alteration of line should be either gradual or obvious. If we look again at **13**, we can see that the flow of line is constant from the base to the shoulder without any obvious deviation until it reaches the shoulder, where it sharply changes in direction toward the rim. The result is an obvious change in direction and break of line. As this change in direction is so sharp, it does not appear out of place but is balanced with the smooth line from the base.

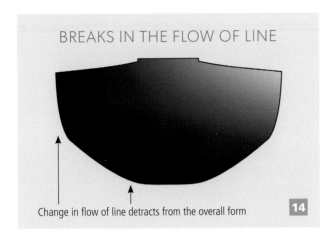

BREAKS IN THE FLOW OF LINE

Change in flow of line detracts from the overall form **14**

If not treated with care, any alteration of line will draw the viewer's eye to this point and detract from the form as a whole. This can be seen in **14**, where the same form is illustrated but with the inclusion of two breaks in the flow of line. This example illustrates how a slight variation of line alters the flow and detracts from the form as a whole.

FORM IS EVERYTHING

Many woods, no matter how beautiful a color when initially turned, will darken or fade due to being exposed to ultraviolet light. Yew (*Taxus buccata*) is a prime example; on first being turned it is bright reddish-brown and white, but will quickly change if placed near a window. Some years ago I turned a small form from yew; the colors were beautifully bright and stunning. Over time the bright reds faded to a deep caramel color, which, while beautiful in its own way, did not resemble the colors when first turned. At such a time, the form will take over, together with any flaws that may initially have been hidden by the busy grain pattern.

Form is everything, so never sacrifice form for the wood. If you have to keep turning away layer upon layer until you achieve a pleasing form, then do just that. If you do not like the idea of turning away exotic or expensive lumber, then practice on unseasoned logs or scrap lumber – anything that is sound and solid will do. Each cut is a gift for us to practice, so make each one count.

HANDY HINT

While you are turning a form, regularly turn off the lathe and take time out to view your project. Stand back from your work and search for areas that might need to be reworked. A good way to test your form is to close your eyes and run your hand over the entire form. Your sense of touch will become more acute and you will notice any subtle changes in line.

BALANCE AND WEIGHT

How often has another woodturner asked, "How thick is the wall?" Of course, we woodturners are inquisitive folk, especially when enquiring about a piece we like; if you have not yet come across this question you certainly will. It is, however, something I have never been asked by anyone outside the world of woodturning. This made me think about why people buy my work. Often at craft fairs my prized thin-walled vase would not sell, as I was told it was not heavy enough to hold flowers, despite me saying that it was not made to hold flowers but simply to be an ornament. I concluded that although woodturners expect a piece to be made in a certain way, very few outside our craft have the same expectations.

I believe that turned work should be made to a high standard of form and finish as well as being balanced in weight for the form. I just want you to think about some of the preconceived ideas that we woodturners have, based on rules set by others. I believe the considerations when making a piece sit into two categories: essential and preferred.

Essential considerations are those that directly affect the successful completion of a project. An example might be the thickness of wall left when rough-turning a form from unseasoned wood. In this case, you have no choice but to adhere to essential factors, or the project will end in failure due to the form cracking or distorting beyond recovery during seasoning, as discussed in Chapter 2.

Preferred considerations are those of personal preference that have no adverse effect on the completion of the project. An example would be the turning of seasoned wood to produce a vase for holding tall grasses. You might decide that the form is only drilled out without hollowing to a thin wall, as weight is needed for stability. While this may not be how others would produce their form, it will have no effect on the successful completion of the project due to the wood being seasoned and stable from the start.

How heavy or thick I leave the wall of a form – other than for items of utility – depends on the balance of weight to form. If a piece appears delicate, I will produce it to feel delicate in weight. If it is a large form, I leave enough material to complement the size and to give it a bit of weight. However, you should find your own way of working outside of applying the essential factors. Some prefer light forms; others prefer chunky forms. If you are thinking of selling your work, it is worth considering that others may have preconceived ideas of what to expect when picking up one of your pieces.

EXAMPLES OF SHAPES

So far form has been illustrated through its separate parts, proportion and line, and how these are put together as a whole.

Within this section is a selection of forms. Some of these are similar to those produced within the seven projects later in the book; you can refer back to the various sections that relate directly to the projects. Others are a development or an alternative design that you may want to try after completing the initial projects.

The selection shown is by no means definitive, but is intended to give a starting point. Each design can be developed and altered to suit your own style, or you can copy them as they are shown. You could photocopy them and display them on a wall near your lathe as a visual aid.

The illustrations are shown in monochrome to be devoid of all other visual information other than shape.

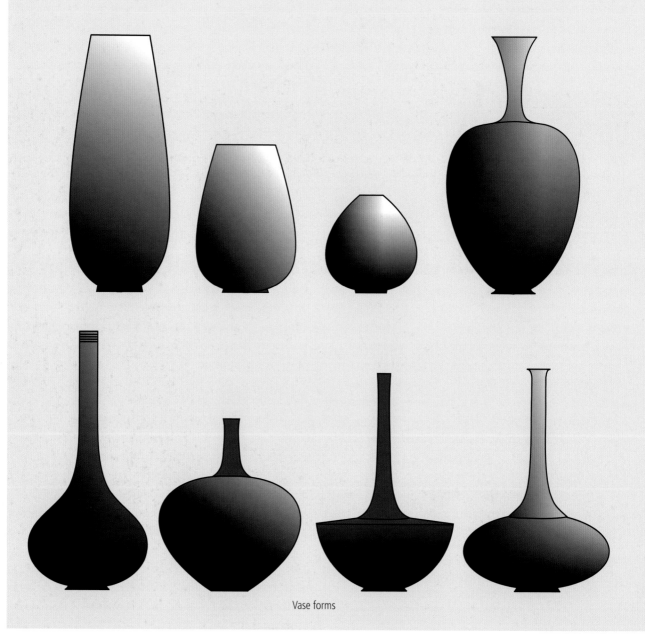

Vase forms

Forms showing a progression in height with the largest diameter located using the rule of thirds

Forms illustrating a progression from the sphere to the squashed sphere

HANDY HINT

Over time, your likes and dislikes within your own work will change. Keep a photographic record and notes as a resource for reviewing your work. This is especially useful if a piece is no longer at hand for viewing. It is often the only record available of your progress. Use your pictures as a study to help you to work out what to change in your future work.

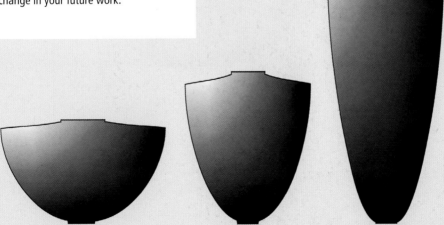

Forms illustrating a single curve from the base to the shoulder with an acute change in direction toward the rim, breaking the rule of thirds

TEMPLATES FOR FORMS

As I have mentioned, a beautiful form will enhance a bland piece of wood, but a beautiful piece of wood will not enhance a poor form. I always advocate form and finish over all other aspects such as grain, color or other adornment. If you get the form right, a piece will have immediate impact even if viewed from afar.

With form being our primary concern at the lathe, the templates here can be used as an aid when you first start turning your forms. It will take you longer to turn a form using a template because you need to start and stop the lathe to offer up the template. Print off the templates, scaling them for the size of form you want in relation to the size of wood you have selected. Stick the template to a piece of card and cut out the negative space. The template can then be offered up to the form with the lathe stopped as an aid to turning.

The templates contained here have been produced so that the smallest form to the left of a group can be produced using a 3-in. (75mm)-high x 6-in. (150mm)-diameter seasoned blank. The remaining templates require larger stock lumber and will have to be roughed or turned to finished size from unseasoned wood; seasoned blanks are generally only available to a maximum thickness of 3½–4 in. (90–100mm).

Scale the templates up or down using a photocopier or scanner. If you have access to a computer, you can scan and crop the templates to their extremities. Copy and paste or load these into a graphics software package and scale the templates to suit your project size.

The illustrations show how the templates can be used, taking into account the tenon or tail center during turning.

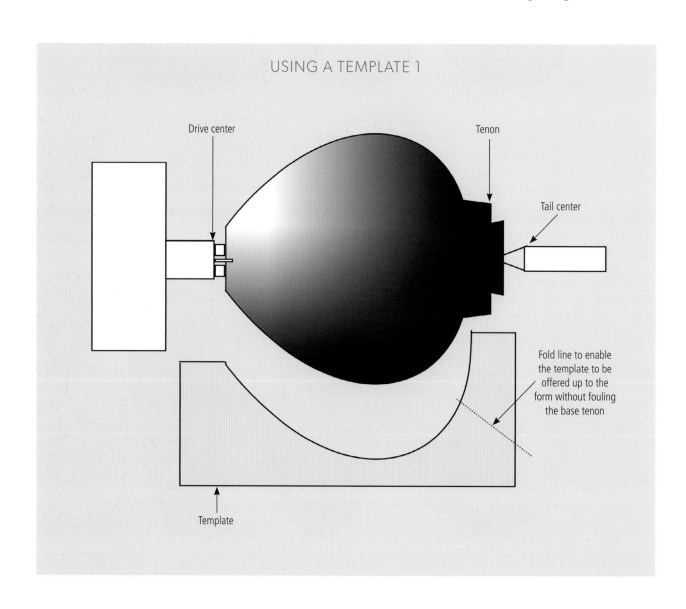

USING A TEMPLATE 1

Drive center

Tenon

Tail center

Fold line to enable the template to be offered up to the form without fouling the base tenon

Template

TURNING HOLLOW FORMS

1 Enclosed form templates

2, 3 & 4 Hollow form templates

1

2

3

4

CHAPTER FIVE

PROJECTS

These projects are progressive and varied in both process and tool techniques. Some utilize unseasoned wood and others seasoned, although all of the projects can be turned using seasoned wood if you wish. However, I would urge you to explore the use of unseasoned wood as it opens up many more possibilities. It is also my belief that to become proficient in our craft the wood we use can only be truly understood when worked in its raw state. I would also encourage you to experiment with the designs. Play around with the ideas and alter them as you want.

This project takes you through the process of turning a deep vessel that has a large opening, allowing you good access and view for hollowing. It is a great form with which to start learning how to turn deeper, as you can easily see what is happening at the cutting tip and how this translates up the tool into the handle. The form is turned to finish size in one go with a thin wall, then oiled and seasoned. You could also first rough-turn the form oversize, fully season it, then re-mount and finish it. Also included in this project are the methods used for finishing a similar rough-turned form (see page 95).

PROJECT ONE
ENCLOSED FORM

ENCLOSED FORM

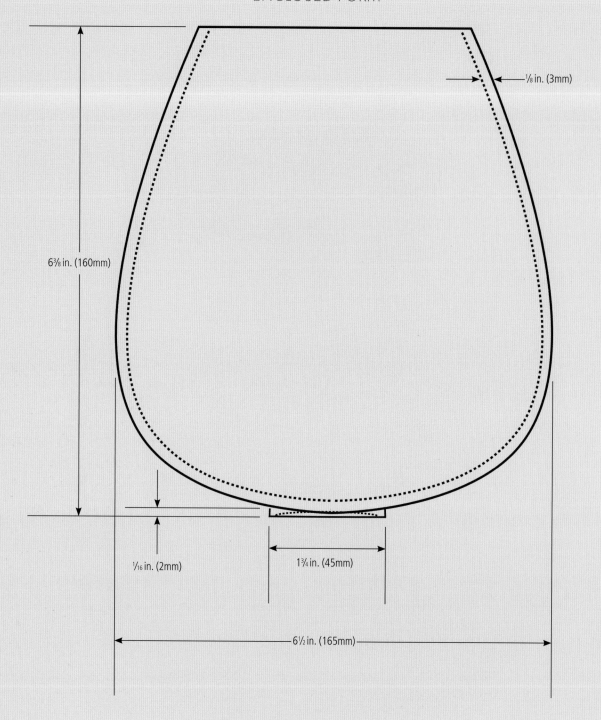

6³⁄₈ in. (160mm)

¹⁄₈ in. (3mm)

¹⁄₁₆ in. (2mm)

1³⁄₄ in. (45mm)

6¹⁄₂ in. (165mm)

TOOLS AND MATERIALS
- 1 x unseasoned piece of oak *(Quercus robur)*, pith included normal wood, 8 in. (200mm) length x 7 in. (180mm) diameter
- 1-in. (25mm) spindle roughing gouge ● ³⁄₈-in. (10mm) bowl gouge with long grind ● ¹⁄₄-in. (6mm) point tool
- ¹⁄₄-in. (6mm) spindle gouge with fingernail grind ● 1-in. (25mm) skew chisel ● Shielded ring-hollowing tool
- 1-in. (25mm) round-nose scraper ● 1-in. (25mm) square-end scraper ● ¹⁄₂-in. (12mm) skew chisel

ORDER/AREA OF CUTS FOR HOLLOWING

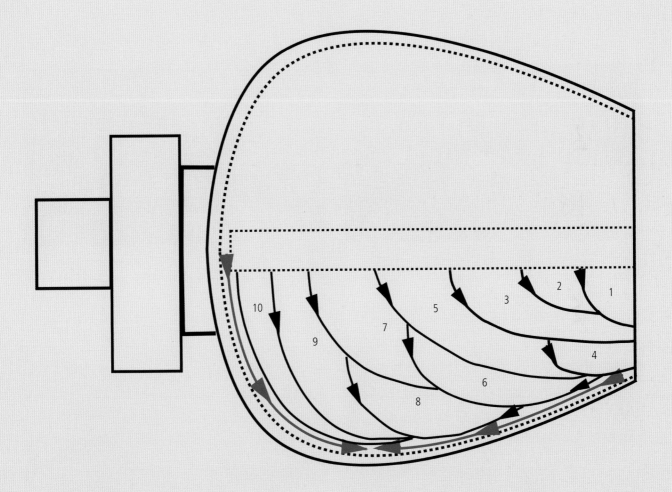

Key

▶ = Direction of areas and direction for roughing cuts

▶ = Direction of finishing cuts and direction for scraping

1 Mount the log with the pith aligned centrally with the drive and tail center. Lock off the drive center and remove any loose bark with a large screwdriver.

2 Using a 1-in. (25mm) spindle roughing gouge, rough to the round.

3 Using a ⅜-in. (10mm) bowl gouge, clean up the front face, producing a tenon to a diameter to suit the jaws of your chuck and a waste area approximately 2 in. (50mm) left of the tenon.

4 Refine the tenon to match the chuck jaw profile using a ½-in. (12mm) skew chisel horizontal on the tool rest with the tip trailing in scraping mode.

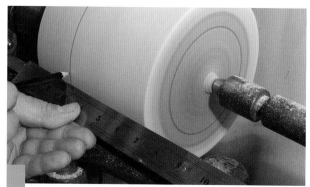

5 Reverse and mount the blank into the chuck. Using a pencil and rule, mark the location of the belly of the form to be one-third the height of the blank – in this instance, 3 in. (75mm) up from the base. Mark the outside diameter of the rim on the front face to be two-thirds the diameter of the blank.

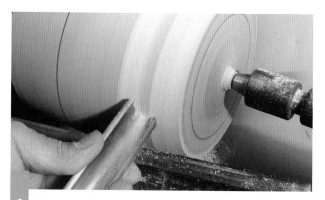

6 Using a 1-in. (25mm) roughing gouge, rough down the material to the right of the line marked, working downhill to a safe distance from the tail center.

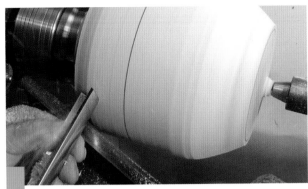

7 Continue with the roughing gouge, producing the profile from the belly to the rim and stopping at a safe distance from the chuck.

8 Change to a ⅜-in. (10mm) bowl gouge or large spindle gouge to refine the profile down into the waste area. Roll the tool over counter-clockwise on reaching the shoulder so that the flutes are horizontal and in scraping mode to prevent the unsupported edge from catching.

9 Use a 1-in. (25mm) skew chisel to refine the line. Again, working downhill from the belly to the rim and base, aim for one continuous, flowing line.

10 Measure the height of the form from the rim to the joint of the base and the waste area. Subtract ⅜ in. (10mm) from this and mark it on the shaft of a sawtooth bit or the barrel of the tailstock, as marked here in blue. Drill to this line using a 1-in. (25mm) sawtooth bit held in the tail center or with a Jacobs chuck. Retract the drill bit regularly to clear the shavings and prevent binding.

11 With the depth hole drilled you can start hollowing. By entering the hole with the cutting tip of your tool you can efficiently peel the fibers as you cut outward. Here I am using a shielded ring-hollowing tool. Open out the entrance of the form, initially leaving the wall around ½ in. (12mm) thick and hollowing to 3 in. (75mm) into the form. Check the diagram on page 89 for the sequence and direction of cuts for this and the following hollowing processes.

HANDY HINT

As you hollow, take note of your senses: listen to and feel the cut, take note of the sound and sensations through the tool handle. The wood will tell you whether your tool presentation is correct as it will cut with relative ease, depending on the type of wood. If you have to fight with the tool, or the wood is not cutting, check your tool presentation; if this appears to be correct, check that the cutting tip is sharp and set correctly. Assuming that you are using sound wood, it will generally only be one of these two issues that will cause you problems.

12 Once the bulk has been removed, continue reducing the wall thickness to ⅛ in. (3mm) for the first 3 in. (75mm) depth inside the form. Check with callipers to make sure the wall is of a consistent thickness.

13 Using a 1-in. (25mm) round-nose scraper, finish the first section A, stopping short of the thicker wall section B.

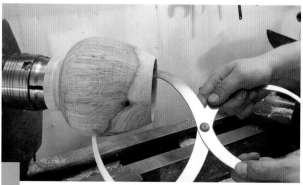

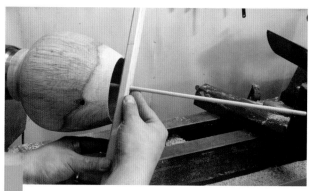

14 Continue with the hollowing tool and scraper, working in stages into the form and checking the wall thickness as you proceed.

15 Check the depth. I use a homemade depth gauge from a dowel and a strip of scrap wood into which a hole is drilled to take the dowel.

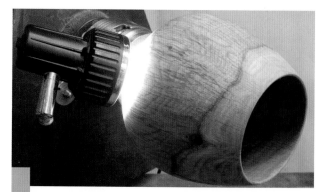

16 Offer the depth gauge up to the outside of the form, holding the straight edge across the base of the form to show the thickness left in the base.

17 To gauge the thickness of the base, an LED light can be positioned to shine on the belly and base of the form. The amount of light penetrating the wall will depend on the translucency of the wood being turned. Continue with the hollowing tool, taking fine cuts until the light penetrating the wood is the same brightness from the belly into the base. Use low-voltage or battery LED lights purpose-built to be used in a workshop environment, making sure that any cables are placed well away from any moving parts of the lathe. Finally, refine the finish in the base with the scraper; if your tool will not reach safely, you can swap to a scraping attachment for your hollowing tool. If you do not have one of these, simply finish the base with abrasive as in step 20.

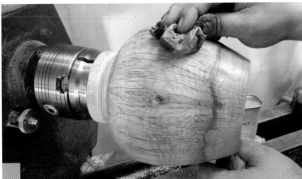

18 Apply thin finishing oil to the inside and outside of the form, wiping away any excess. Applying oil to the wood reduces dust during finishing and helps keep heat to a minimum by acting as a lubricant between the abrasive and the wood.

19 Finish the outside with abrasive from 100 to 320 grit – here this was done by hand. Keep moving the abrasive back and forth to prevent inducing radial lines on the surface. If the wood starts to dry out or you feel heat coming through the abrasive, stop the lathe and apply more oil. Finishing with oil will clog the abrasive but there is no need to throw it away. Refresh the abrasive by placing it face up on a flat surface and using a small bronze brush to clean out the oil and wood fibers from the grit.

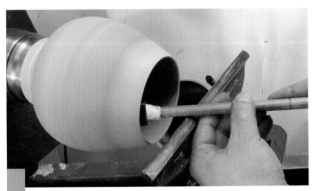

20 Finish the inside of the form with abrasive from 100 to 320 grit by fixing abrasive to a piece of dowel long enough to reach to the base of the form.

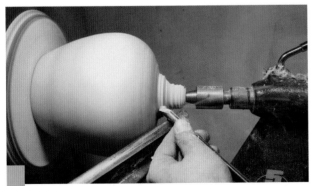

21 Remove from the chuck and mount between a friction plate and the tail center. The friction plate here is simply a plywood disk with a tenon made from waste wood screwed to the back to fit the chuck. High-density rubber (in this case an old car mat) was cut to shape and stuck to the surface of the plywood, giving grip and allowing the rim to sink into the rubber with moderate pressure applied from the tail center. The rubber is covered with masking tape to protect the rim of the form being turned. Use a ⅜-in. (10mm) bowl gouge with a long grind to reduce the tenon down to the diameter of the intended foot – in this instance, 1¾ in. (45mm).

22 Use a ¼-in. (6mm) spindle gouge to reduce the waste further to around ⅜ in. (10mm); leave approximately ¹⁄₁₆-in. (2mm) for the foot. This gives the form lift when displayed and allows the line of the form to flow continually around without the distraction of intersecting with the surface on which it has been placed. This is my preference, but if you prefer a different style of foot, alter as you wish.

23 Using a ¼-in. (6mm) point tool with the tip trailing, produce two grooves for decoration in the base of the foot.

24 Stop the lathe and cut through the remaining waste with a fine-tooth saw blade.

25 Blend the remaining waste with a power carver or sharp chisel, cutting away from your body.

26 Refine the base with abrasive attached to a small sanding arbor fixed into a waste piece of wood turned to fit your chuck jaws. Refine down to 240 grit, taking care not to alter the rim of the foot. Finish by hand in line with the grain with 320-grit abrasive.

27 Apply a final coat of finishing oil, wiping away any excess. Place into a plastic bag, leaving the top open, and follow the instructions for seasoning a thin-walled form (see page 156).

28 After seasoning (which took around three weeks in this case), the form is ready to accept the final finish. First, buff the outside to prepare the surface. Apply several coats of finishing oil to both the inside and outside of the form, with any excess wiped away. After the oil has dried, buff the surface by hand with a soft cloth to produce a natural, low-satin finish.

FINISHING A ROUGH-TURNED FORM

After seasoning, your form can be finish-turned. The process to achieve this is fairly simple, as the bulk of the work has been done already. We first need to re-establish the tenon and shoulder for a good fit for the jaws of your chuck. Bowls, enclosed forms or hollow forms are all approached in the same way.

I have used these methods for many years; the only tools needed are the producing of friction drives from scrap wood to suit the forms that require finishing. Once made, these drives can be used time and time again, and therefore make a cheap, simple and effective method.

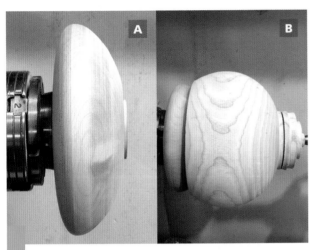

29 Mount the form between a conical friction drive, supporting the rim and bringing up the tail center to apply moderate pressure. Here the drive is simply a scrap hollow form that was kept for this purpose. **A** shows a drive turned to have convex surfaces on both sides as well as a tenon on each, which allows it to be reversed to suit differing forms. The convex surfaces allow for cuts to continue past the edge of the rim while giving maximum support to the form – see **B**.

30 Refine the shoulder of the waste wood using a ¼-in. (6mm) spindle gouge.

31 Use a ½-in. (12mm) skew chisel horizontal on the tool rest with the tip trailing to refine the tenon for the chuck jaws.

32 Using a ⅜-in. (10mm) bowl gouge, refine the profile, working downhill toward the tail center. However, if a cross-grain form were being finished, the direction of cut would be taken from the tail center out to the rim.

33 Refine the top section of the profile to the rim, again working downhill.

34 Refine the surface with a 1-in. (25mm) square-end scraper.

35 Finish with abrasive from 120 to 320 grit.

36 Clean up the rim with a push cut using a ⅜-in. (10mm) bowl gouge. There will be some breakout on the inside of the rim, but this will be turned away when turning out the inside.

37 Hollow the inside, working in sections as with the main project.

38 Refine the surface with a 1-in. (25mm) round-nose scraper. Finish with abrasive and apply your preferred finish at this stage to the inside, rim and main body or continue and apply the finish off the lathe.

39 Using a ⅜-in. (10mm) bowl gouge, reduce the waste at the base and produce a foot as before.

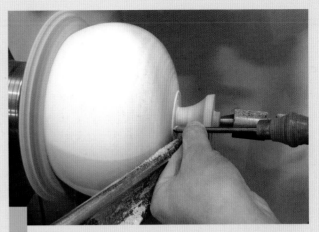

40 Add detail to the foot with a ¼-in. (6mm) point tool. Reduce the waste section further to around ⅜ in. (10mm) diameter with a spindle gouge. Stop the lathe and cut through the remaining waste with a fine-tooth saw blade. Finish with a power carver and abrasive as before.

In this project, I will show you how to make a small hollow form using an offcut of seasoned end-grain yew branch wood. Small pieces like this one, up to 4 in. (100mm) in height, can be hollowed quite easily with a ¼-in. (6mm) or ⅜-in. (10mm) spindle gouge ground with a fingernail profile. Hollowing is made easier by producing a tenon on the top of the form, which is parted off to enable easy tool access through a larger hole. The parted tenon is then reinserted into a recess and the joint disguised with simple grooves using a point tool.

PROJECT TWO
INSERT HOLLOW FORM

INSERT HOLLOW FORM

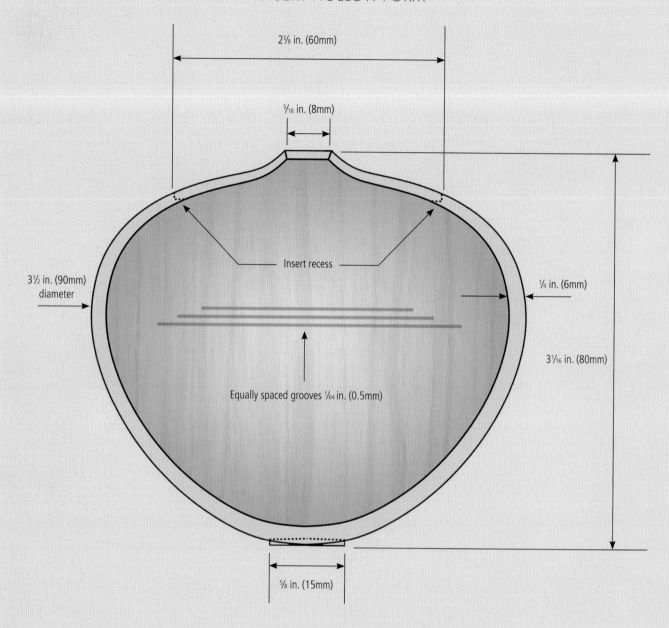

2³⁄₈ in. (60mm)

⁵⁄₁₆ in. (8mm)

Insert recess

3¹⁄₂ in. (90mm) diameter

¹⁄₄ in. (6mm)

3¹⁄₁₆ in. (80mm)

Equally spaced grooves ¹⁄₆₄ in. (0.5mm)

⁵⁄₈ in. (15mm)

TOOLS AND MATERIALS

- 1 x piece of end-grain yew *(Taxus baccata)* or any close-grain wood, 5¹⁄₈ in. (130mm) length x 4 in. (100mm) diameter
- 1-in. (25mm) spindle roughing gouge • ¹⁄₂-in. (12mm) skew chisel • ³⁄₈-in. (10mm) spindle gouge
- ¹⁄₄-in. (6mm) spindle gouge • ¹⁄₄-in. (6mm) parting tool • ¹⁄₄-in. (6mm) point tool • ¹⁄₈-in. (3mm) parting tool
- 1-in. (25mm) square-end scraper

SUPPLEMENTARY TOOLS AND SUNDRIES

- Abrasives from 120 to 400 grit • Finishing oil • Fine-tooth saw • 1-in. (25mm) sawtooth bit • Power carver
- Medium-viscosity CA glue

1 Mount the blank between centers. Using a 1-in. (25mm) spindle roughing gouge, rough to the round.

2 Use a ¼-in. (6mm) parting tool to clean up the face at the tailstock end of the blank and produce a tenon to suit the jaws of your chuck. Continue along from the tenon to produce a waste area approximately ⅜ in. (10mm) wide.

3 Reverse the blank into the chuck and tighten, bringing the tail center up for added support and security. Repeat the same process to produce a second tenon, but this time producing a waste area approximately ¾ in. (20mm) wide. This is the top of the project and will be later parted from the blank to allow for hollowing.

4 Using a ⅜-in. (10mm) spindle gouge, produce the basic profile of the form working from the outside diameter in – stop just short of the waste area.

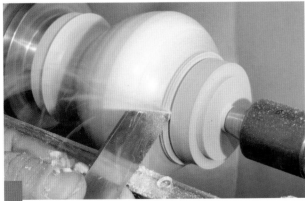

5 Using a ⅛-in. (3mm) parting tool, part into the insert leaving a small amount of material as a registration to aid in the production of a recess to enable the parted section to be inserted after hollowing. Stop short of parting all the way through here and stop the lathe.

6 You can now cut through the remaining waste with a fine-tooth saw blade, taking care not to mark the top face of the form. If the grain is not obvious, mark a line on the edge of the insert and the top of the form for alignment later.

7 Measure the height of the form to the joint with the waste area near the base; subtract ⅜ in. (10mm) from this and mark it on a 1-in. (25mm) sawtooth bit or similar. Drill to depth using the marked line as a gauge.

8 Using a ⅜-in. (10mm) spindle gouge, hollow the entrance hole leaving a shoulder approximately ¼ in. (6mm) wide. Hollow to a depth of three-quarters the height of the insert previously parted off – when blending the top of the form, you want to have enough material to achieve your desired shape.

9 Using a ¼-in. (6mm) parting tool, part into the shoulder and work up to the registration mark/edge that was left from the parted insert. Taper the cut, slightly angling in as you progress deeper, removing small amounts and stopping regularly to offer up the insert. Repeat this process until the insert just starts into the recess.

10 Next, using the toe of a ½-in. (12mm) skew chisel horizontal on the tool rest with the tip trailing, slightly refine and parallel the recess until you have a good fit with the previously parted insert.

HANDY HINTS

The grooves used for this hollow form could be replaced with coves, if you prefer. To achieve this, use the radius point of a small spindle gouge in trailing mode.

Remember to turn the lathe speed down when finishing with fine abrasives on dense lumber such as this. Any excess heat caused during the finishing process can induce heat checks or fine cracks in the end grain.

11 Hollow out the inside of the form using a ⅜-in. (10mm) spindle gouge, leaving thickness in the base of the recess. Work from inside out with the tool horizontal on the tool rest with the flutes at 45°. The cut should be at 10–11 o'clock. Do not be tempted to cut uphill into the base – you do not want to cut into the end grain, but rather peel from inside out. Due to the size of the opening, the shoulder for hollowing is not a problem using a spindle gouge; alternatively, you can use a small hollowing tool.

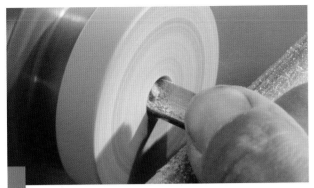

12 Place the insert into the chuck and tighten via the tenon produced. Use a ¼-in. (6mm) spindle gouge with a fingernail profile to drill out the center of the insert. To do this, set the tool at center height, the flutes at 45° and push into the center. Alternatively, you could use a small drill held via a Jacobs chuck in the tailstock to produce the hole.

13 Continuing with the ¼-in. (6mm) spindle gouge, peel outward from the hole and concave the underside of the insert, stopping around 5/16 in. (5mm) from the outside edge. Hollowing the underside of the insert will lighten the appearance of the opening. If you prefer, you can leave this section and glue the insert back into the form simply drilled through.

14 Remount the main form into the chuck and run a small amount of medium-viscosity CA glue around the inside of the recess. Fit the insert into place, lining up the grain, and bring up the tail center to apply light pressure while it cures.

15 Using a ⅜-in. (10mm) spindle gouge, blend the form from the shoulder into the neck flowing up to the opening, aiming for a wall thickness at the rim of around 5/64 in. (2mm).

16 Using a 1-in. (25mm) square-end scraper, refine the surface of the form. I used a shear scraper with the tool edge presented at 45° to the wood. Once satisfied, finish the top two-thirds of the form with abrasive from 120 to 320 grit, making sure you use suitable dust extraction and a face mask.

17 Use a ¼-in. (6mm) point tool to produce equally spaced grooves. Start with the center of the first groove at the joint; this will hide any visible line in the base of the groove. Work toward the opening, stopping around 5/16 in. (5mm) from the rim to produce a small area to frame the hole.

18 Clean up the edges of the grooves by giving a light sand with 400-grit abrasive. If the point tool is kept sharp, then the grooves will have been cut clean with little finishing required.

19 Reverse the form between the tail center and a friction drive in the chuck. Produce a concave friction drive that sits over the rim or opening without coming into contact with it. Any undue pressure will cause the rim to crack, so drive the form via the top/face. Using a ³⁄₈-in. (10mm) spindle gouge, refine the base of the form into the waste area.

20 Next, reduce the waste adjacent to the base using a ¹⁄₄-in. (6mm) parting tool; this allows room to continue with the ¹⁄₄-in. (6mm) point tool. Continue producing grooves all the way down to the base and finish with 400-grit abrasive as before.

21 Using a ¹⁄₈-in. (3mm) parting tool, part in at the base, angling the cut to produce a concave surface so the form will sit stable. Turn the lathe speed down to around 300 rpm to do this, leaving around ⁵⁄₁₆ in. (5mm) waste, and stop the lathe. Cut through the remaining waste with a fine-tooth saw blade as before.

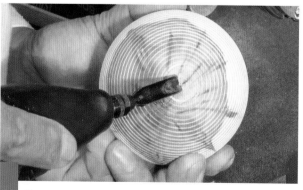

22 Use a power carver to clean up the base, working away from your body. Refine this area by hand with abrasive down to 400 grit.

23 Apply a thin finishing oil, wipe off any excess and allow to dry. Here I used lemon oil as it is thin and soaks into the wood without clogging the base of the grooves. Once dry, simply buff by hand with a soft cloth.

HANDY HINT
When blending the underside concave profile of the insert, leave enough material to allow for profiling the top after the insert has been glued back in place. Removing too much material from the underneath can mean that you cut through the wall when profiling the top of the form. For the first two or three forms you try, leave the underside a little thicker until you get the hang of it.

This project takes you through the turning of a small form that is hollowed through the base. A section is parted from the base of the form, allowing greater tool access for hollowing. Then the parted section is glued back in place with the grain aligned. The joint is disguised by the addition of small grooves. For this project, I chose a pre-cut blank of spalted beech, 4 in. (100mm) in length and 5 in. (125mm) in diameter. The form could also be turned using 4- x 4-in. (100 x 100mm)-square parallel-grain seasoned stock to produce a more vertical form.

PROJECT THREE
HOLLOW FORM TURNED THROUGH THE BASE

HOLLOW FORM TURNED THROUGH THE BASE

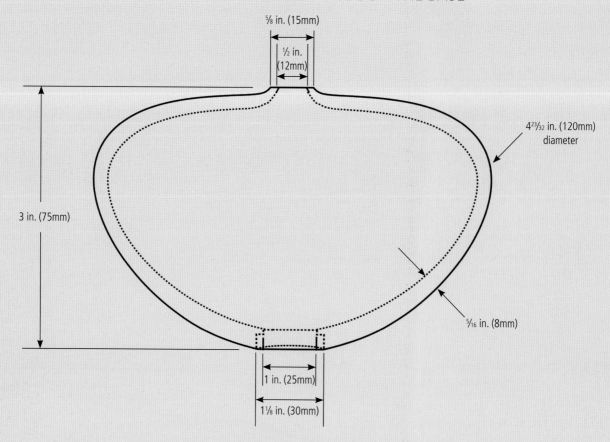

5/8 in. (15mm)

1/2 in. (12mm)

4²³/₃₂ in. (120mm) diameter

3 in. (75mm)

5/16 in. (8mm)

1 in. (25mm)

1⅛ in. (30mm)

SEQUENCE OF CUTS

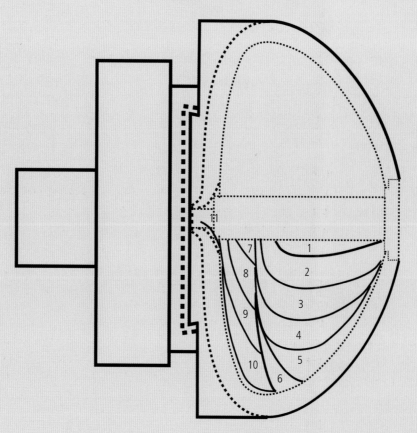

HOLLOW FORM THROUGH BASE

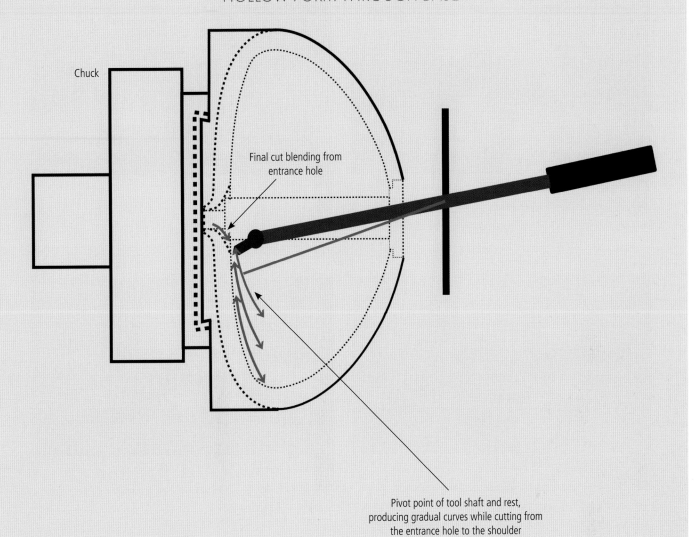

Chuck

Final cut blending from
entrance hole

Pivot point of tool shaft and rest,
producing gradual curves while cutting from
the entrance hole to the shoulder

TOOLS AND MATERIALS

- 1 x pre-seasoned blank of cross-grain spalted beech *(Fagus sylvatica)*, 4 in. (100mm) length x 5 in. (125mm) diameter
- ³⁄₈-in. (10mm) bowl gouge with long grind ● ¹⁄₄-in. (6mm) spindle gouge with fingernail grind
- 1-in. (25mm) square-end scraper ● ¹⁄₂-in. (12mm) skew chisel ● ¹⁄₂-in. (12mm)-diameter shaft hollowing tool
- ¹⁄₄-in. (6mm) parting tool ● ¹⁄₄-in. (6mm) point tool ● ¹⁄₈-in. (3mm) parting tool

SUPPLEMENTARY TOOLS AND SUNDRIES

- Sanding sealer ● Your preferred wax finish ● Abrasives from 120 to 320 grit ● Power carver
- 8-in. (200mm)-diameter open-weave buffing pad and arbor ● White diamond buffing compound
- Medium-viscocity CA glue ● Paper towel or similar ● Fine-tooth saw ● Vernier calipers ● ¹⁄₂-in. (12mm) sawtooth bit

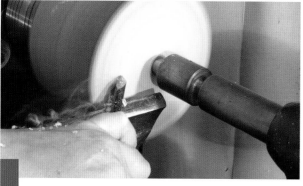

1 Mount the blank on a ⅜-in. (10mm) screw chuck or similar and with the tail center in place for added security clean-up. Using a ⅜-in. (10mm) bowl gouge, clean up the front face with a pull cut from the tail center out.

2 Clean up the outside of the blank using the ⅜-in. (10mm) bowl gouge.

3 Produce a tenon to suit the jaws of your chuck, in this instance, 2-in. (50mm)-diameter dovetail profile jaws. Turn a shoulder approximately ⅜ in. (10mm) larger in diameter and ½ in. (12mm) wide to the left of the tenon. This is for the chuck jaws to sit up against, but it will also be parted off once refined for reinserting into the base after the inside has been hollowed.

4 Refine the tenon to achieve a good fit with the chuck jaw profile. Here a ½-in. (12mm) skew chisel was used horizontal on the tool rest with the tip trailing in scraping mode.

5 Reverse the blank and tighten into the jaws via the tenon previously turned. Produce a second tenon with the ⅜-in. (10mm) bowl gouge, again to suit the chuck jaws on what will end up being the top of the form. This tenon need only be ¼ in. (6mm) deep into the face.

6 Using a ¼-in. (6mm) spindle gouge with a fingernail profile, clean up the hole used for the screw chuck to remove any sign of the cut thread, blending the opening outward as you cut. This leads the eye down into the hole and softens the rim. Here the flutes of the gouge are held at 45° and the cutting edge is just left of 12 o'clock trailing with the tool being gently pulled out.

7 Again, remove from the chuck, reversing onto the tenon turned in step 4, and tighten. Draw a line on the outside of the form one-third down from the top of the tenon held in the chuck jaws – this being the location of the shoulder. Using a ⅜-in. (10mm) bowl gouge, rough out the form starting from the shoulder up toward the line. Aim to produce a smooth curve, tightening as you reach the shoulder.

8 Continue with the bowl gouge by continuing and refining the base line of the form into the area to be parted off. You will need to cut against the grain to do this; this is not a problem, as the final refining/finishing cuts will be performed from the base out after the hollowing process.

9 Using a ¼-in. (6mm) parting tool, part into the shoulder to a diameter of 1¼ in. (30mm). Make a second part to the right of the first, producing a parallel tenon approximately ½ in. (12mm) wide. This will be parted off and reinserted into the base later.

10 Using a ⅛-in. (3mm) parting tool, part into the tenon previously turned. Leave a small registration of the tenon on the base of the form as a guide for producing the recess. (A close-up of this can be seen in step 12.) Stop short of parting all the way through and stop the lathe.

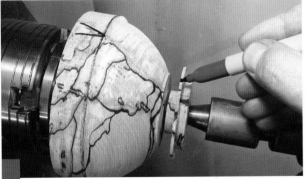

11 Mark one line on the outer edge of the waste area of the tenon and one line at the shoulder – here indicated by a blue V-shaped arrow. This is to help line up both parts when the tenon is reinserted into the base. It is not so essential on spalted wood as the markings are pronounced, but it is a good practice to adopt, especially on plain close-grain woods as it can be difficult to match up the two parts without such guide marks. Once marked, either twist off the tenon if you have parted in or cut through the remaining waste with a fine-tooth saw blade.

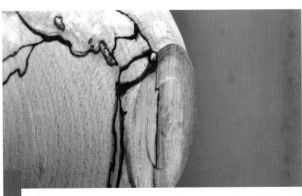

12 Here you can see a close-up of the base showing the registration material left after parting.

13 Using vernier calipers, measure from the top of the form (including the tenon) to the base.

14 Subtract ½ in. (12mm) from this measurement and mark it on the shaft of a ½-in. (12mm) sawtooth bit with a permanent marker. Drill out to this line marked on the drill.

15 Using a ¼-in. (6mm) parting tool, part into the base with a plunge cut, staying inside the registration mark. Angle the tool in toward the center of the form as you cut to produce a tapered hole. Produce the hole to a depth approximately the same height as the tenon previously removed.

16 Using a ½-in. (12mm)-diameter shaft hollowing tool with a small scraping tip, open out the drilled hole slightly, leaving a small shoulder. Then hollow out the inside of the form, opening out from the base. Follow the outside profile as you progress up to the shoulder, aiming for a wall thickness of around ⅜ in. (10mm) and leaving material for blending the outside profile later. On reaching the shoulder, hollow out from the entrance hole using the ½-in. (12mm) step produced during the drilling process as a guide for depth. Produce a gradual curve from the entrance hole to the shoulder, using the intersection of the tool shaft and rest as a pivot point. The diagrams on pages 108–109 clarify the sequence of cuts as well as the process for hollowing from the step to the shoulder.

17 Stop and check the wall thickness regularly. If you are concerned about how deep you are going in relation to the top, take the form, stop the lathe, and shine a small light up inside the form using the step from the drill bit as a guide.

18 Once hollowed, open out the recess to accept the tenon previously parted from the base. Take fine cuts using the toe of a ½-in. (12mm) skew held horizontal on the tool rest with the tip trailing, angling the tool as before as you approach the registration mark.

19 Check regularly for fit. Once the tenon fits at the entrance to the recess, continue with the skew as before, but this time parallel the recess until you have a good, snug fit with the insert.

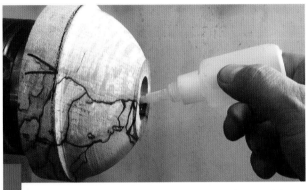

20 With the lathe stationary, apply medium-viscosity CA glue around the inside of the recess.

21 Fit the insert, making sure the grain is lined up before pressing home. Bring the tail center into the indent previously left to apply moderate pressure and make sure the insert fits flush with the internal shoulder. Allow to dry.

22 Using the skew as before, refine any mismatch at the tenon before reversing into the chuck jaws.

23 Reverse the form into the chuck, making sure it runs true before tightening. You are now relying on a glue joint as you turn, so bring up the tail center into the entrance hole, protecting the surface of the form using a small piece of folded paper towel between the two. Using a ⅜-in. (10mm) bowl gouge, shape the top from the rim; I used a pull cut initially, transitioning into a push cut as I neared the shoulder. Blend the form into the shoulder, producing a curve to match the one that flows from the base up.

24 Refine the surface from the rim to the shoulder using a 1-in. (25mm) square-end scraper. Here I angled the tool for a shear scrape.

25 Remove the tail center and finish the inside of the rim with abrasive rolled tightly from 120 to 320 grit. Make sure you wear adequate respiratory protection as well as using air extraction at source.

26 Continue to finish the top to the shoulder to 320-grit abrasive. Here I used an inertia sanding arbor, but you can finish by hand if you prefer – just remember to keep the abrasive moving across the surface to prevent radial lines.

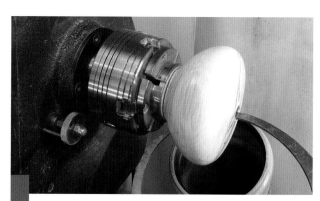

27 Check the thickness at the base one last time. If all has gone well, you should have around ⅜ in. (10mm) remaining, leaving enough for blending the lower section into the foot.

28 Produce a cone-shaped friction drive from waste wood to fit into the hole of the form. Tighten the drive into the chuck and sandwich the form onto this, protecting the inside of the rim with a paper towel. Bring up the tail center and apply moderate pressure. Using a ⅜-in. (10mm) bowl gouge, reduce the tenon and waste down to a safe distance from the tail center. Blend the flow of line from the joint with the insert up into the form; you should have more than enough material to do this as the wall was left fairly thick in the base.

29 Using a ⅜-in. (10mm) spindle gouge with a long grind, reduce the waste tenon down further, refining and concaving the base. Don't worry if you need to push in with the tool to do this – the grain here is almost horizontal to the foot, so unsupported grain should not be an issue.

30 Using a ¼-in. (6mm) point tool with the tip trailing, disguise the joint: cut several grooves into the base, starting with the first on the joint itself, then cut two more, decreasing in diameter toward the center of the base.

31 Finish the base to the shoulder as before.

32 Cut through the remaining waste with a fine-tooth saw blade, taking care not to mark the base.

33 Blend the remaining waste using a power carver or sharp chisel, always cutting away from your body.

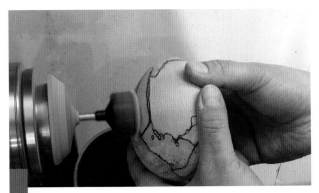

34 Within the friction drive a ¼-in. (6mm) hole has been drilled to accept a small hook-and-loop sanding arbor. Refine the base carefully with 320-grit abrasive.

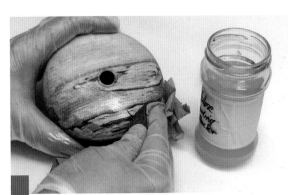

35 Apply sanding sealer, or your preferred oil finish.

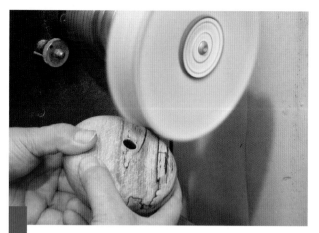

36 Buff the form with a cotton 8-in. (200mm) pad and white diamond compound.

37 Apply several coats of wax with a soft cloth and buff by hand to finish.

HANDY HINTS

Remember when hollowing with a scraping cutter that the cutting edge should be presented to cut on center and trailing as with any scraper to prevent catches.

When entering a form with a scraping cutter, rotate the tool counter-clockwise to around 7 o'clock and gently present the cutting tip to the rotating wood. This results in the forces exerted on the tip being reduced due to the steep trailing angle at which it is presented to the wood. Slowly rotate the cutting tip back toward center height at 9 o'clock until an efficient, controllable cut is achieved. I call this "shaping the cut"; it becomes more valuable the greater the cutting tip overhangs from the tool rest associated with deeper vessels.

For small forms with a steep undercut, choose a thin, pointed scraping tip. The small surface of the tip cuts more efficiently in tight corners because there is less surface area than is associated with larger profiles.

For this project, I wanted to turn a contemporary vase from an end-grain beech (*Fagus sylvatica*) blank that could be used as a visual item on its own, or to display dried or artificial flowers. I wanted to incorporate one of the latest accent colors used in interiors – bright lime – to add a splash of color while leaving a large amount of the natural wood showing. By using your preferred color, the vase can be connected with your interior color scheme. For the coloring of this item I used acrylic spray paint. However, you can just as easily use a paint sample can from a local DIY store. These come in hundreds of shades and you can often get the exact match of a particular color.

PROJECT FOUR
CONTEMPORARY BUD VASE

CONTEMPORARY BUD VASE

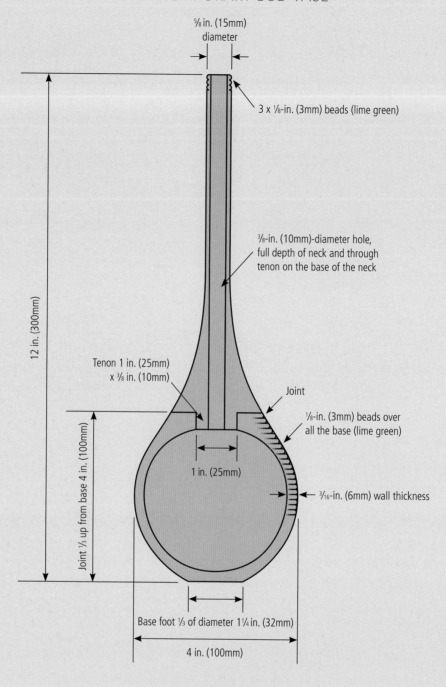

⅝ in. (15mm) diameter

3 x ⅛-in. (3mm) beads (lime green)

⅜-in. (10mm)-diameter hole, full depth of neck and through tenon on the base of the neck

12 in. (300mm)

Tenon 1 in. (25mm) x ⅜ in. (10mm)

Joint

⅛-in. (3mm) beads over all the base (lime green)

Joint ⅓ up from base 4 in. (100mm)

1 in. (25mm)

³⁄₁₆-in. (6mm) wall thickness

Base foot ⅓ of diameter 1¼ in. (32mm)

4 in. (100mm)

TOOLS AND MATERIALS

● 4- x 4- x 14-in. (100 x 100 x 355mm) parallel-grain blank ● ⅝-in. (16mm) scraping hollower ● ¼-in. (6mm) point tool ● ¼-in. (6mm) parting tool ● ⅛-in. (3mm) parting tool ● ½-in. (12mm) skew chisel ● ⅜-in. (10mm) spindle gouge ● 1¼-in. (32mm) spindle roughing gouge ● Callipers ● ¼-in. (6mm) spindle gouge

SUPPLEMENTARY TOOLS AND SUNDRIES

● Fine-tooth saw blade ● Forstner bit ● Jacobs chuck ● ⅜-in. (10mm)-diameter drill bit ● PVA glue ● Abrasives from 120 to 320 grit ● Acrylic sanding sealer ● Your chosen spray ● Acrylic satin lacquer ● Paper towel ● Power carver

1   Take a 4- x 4- x 14-in. (100 x 100 x 355mm) spindle blank and rough
    down to the round between centers using a 1¼-in. (32mm) spindle
roughing gouge.

2   Use a ¼-in. (6mm) parting tool to clean up the front face of the blank
    and produce a tenon on the base to suit your chuck jaws. Then, with a
pencil and rule, mark the main measurements of the form onto the blank. Mark
the base, main shoulder joint, where you would like the neck to blend into the
shoulder, and the top of the vase.

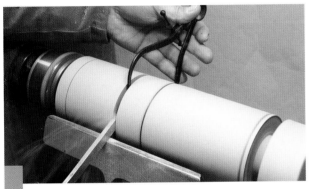

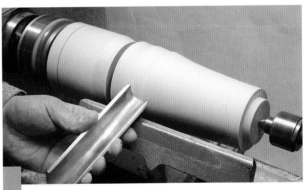

3   Reverse the blank into the chuck, and use calipers set to 2 in. (50mm)
    to part in to depth to denote the top of the vase, leaving a small
amount of waste wood to clean up later. Then, set the calipers to approximately
one-third of the diameter – 1¼ in. (32mm) – and part in at the joint line, which
in this instance is approximately one-third up from the base of the form, to a
width of around ⅜ in. (10mm).

4   Use the parting tool to produce a second tenon at the top of the vase to
    enable the neck to be reversed for drilling. Remove any remaining waste
to the right of the tenon by parting through, removing the tail center for the last
part. Using a 1¼-in. (32mm) spindle roughing gouge, start to blend the shape
from the joint to the top tenon.

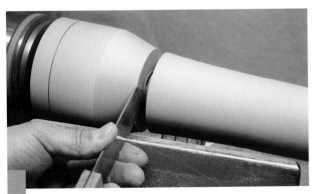

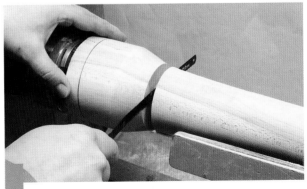

5   Use a ⅛-in. (3mm) parting tool to part into the joint, leaving a
    registration mark on the left face of the form. Part down, leaving
approximately ⅜ in. (10mm) remaining, and then stop the lathe.

6   Remove the remaining waste wood and the vase neck using a
    fine-tooth saw blade.

7 Use a Forstner bit in a Jacobs chuck to drill out the center of the form to the required depth for the project.

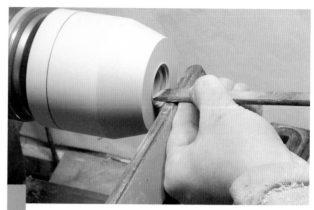

8 Use a ½-in. (12mm) skew chisel, held horizontally in a trailing mode, to open out the hole of the form until the tenon of the neck is a good fit.

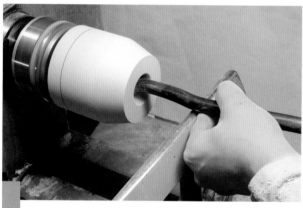

9 Use a ⅝-in. (16mm) scraping hollower to hollow out the main form to lighten the vase.

10 Insert the tenon turned previously on the top of the vase neck into the chuck and drill out the central hole using a standard ⅜-in. (10mm)-diameter drill bit. Drill down to the full depth of the bit. Remove the drill regularly to extract the shavings and to stop the tool from binding.

11 Glue the drilled end of the neck back into the main form using quick-set PVA glue. Bring the running center up to add light pressure while it starts to cure. Alternatively, you can use low-viscosity cyanoacrylate adhesive.

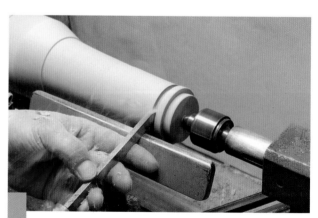

12 Mark the top of the vase with a pencil and rule and part the waste wood off using a ¼-in. (6mm) parting tool. Stop short of the ⅜-in. (10mm) drilled hole. Remove the remainder using a fine-tooth saw blade, as previously shown.

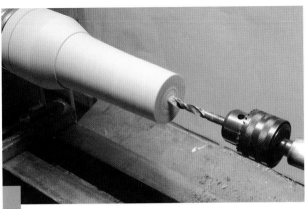

13 Use the ⅜-in. (10mm) drill bit to drill into the neck of the vase. Be sure to go down to the first hole you drilled.

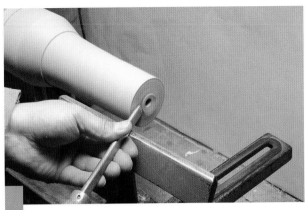

14 Use a ½-in. (12mm) skew chisel to clean up the front face, taking fine cuts due to the overhang of the vase from the chuck.

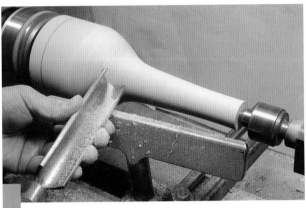

15 Use a 1¼-in. (32mm) spindle roughing gouge to rough down the main shape for the vase from the shoulder.

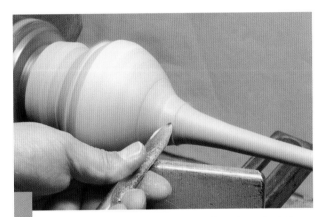

16 Once the main form has been produced, use a ⅜-in. (10mm) spindle gouge to refine the profile from the main shoulder of the form up to the neck of the form. Use the ⅜-in. (10mm) spindle gouge to refine the profile for the base and blend the two together. Sand the form down from 120- to 320-grit abrasive by hand, keeping the abrasive moving over the form to stop radial lines being cut into the surface of the vase. Use direct and ambient air filtration as well as a facemask to shield you from the dust.

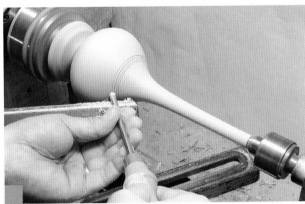

17 Use a ¼-in. (6mm) point tool to produce beads equidistant from the joint line down the base of the form. Turn two beads above the joint to disguise it within the base of the beads. Remove some of the waste wood from the base near the chuck so that the beads can be continued safely toward the base.

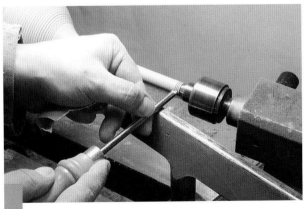

18 Produce three beads at the top of the neck, again using the point tool with the running center in place to add support.

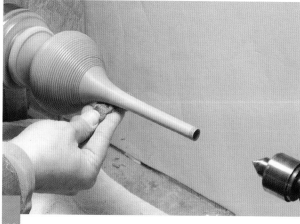

19 Cover the lathe and apply several coats of acrylic sanding sealer. Allow to dry between each coat and, once dry, cut back with steel wool with the lathe running at around 300 rpm.

20 Mask up the form, leaving the beading exposed, cover/protect the lathe and spray the exposed areas with your chosen spray. Allow to dry and repeat the coats until you have good coverage.

21 Allow to dry, and then remove the masking tape. Define the joint line of the beech and colored area by either using fine abrasive or the point tool.

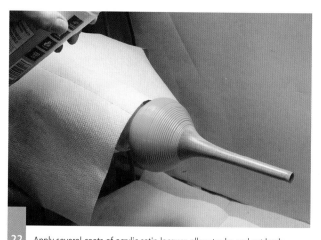

22 Apply several coats of acrylic satin lacquer, allow to dry and cut back, if required, with steel wool; for this, set the lathe speed to around 250 rpm. Reverse the form onto a friction drive and protect the neck with paper towel. Using a ¼-in. (6mm) spindle gouge, reduce the waste section to produce a concave base, leaving about ⅜ in. (10mm) of waste. Stop the lathe and cut through this waste with a fine-tooth saw blade. Blend with a power carver and finish with abrasive from 120–320 grit, as shown on page 94, steps 25–26. Apply sanding sealer and, once dry, apply the color to the exposed area using a fine brush. Once dry, apply several fine coats of acrylic satin lacquer as before.

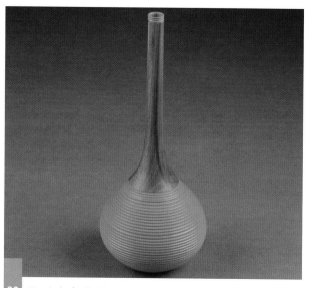

23 Here is the finished bud vase complete with lime green spray paint.

HELPFUL HINT

To add more interest to the colored area, a contrasting color can be painted on and then wiped off the high points using a sponge or paper towel. As an alternative to using spray paint try applying contrasting woods instead. The sky's the limit, so put some of your ideas into practice. For a strong visual display, try making a set of three vases in varying sizes.

This project goes through the process of turning a cross-grain seasoned blank with a steep undercut. This form lends itself to the addition of a lid and finial, and is also an excellent practice form for hollowing steep undercuts. The height of the form can be altered with differing stock, especially when utilizing larger unseasoned stock for rough turning. As with all the forms and projects featured in this book, there are many variations that can be tried, so experiment with the shapes to see what you can come up with.

PROJECT FIVE
SQUAT FORM WITH UNDERCUT

SQUAT FORM WITH UNDERCUT

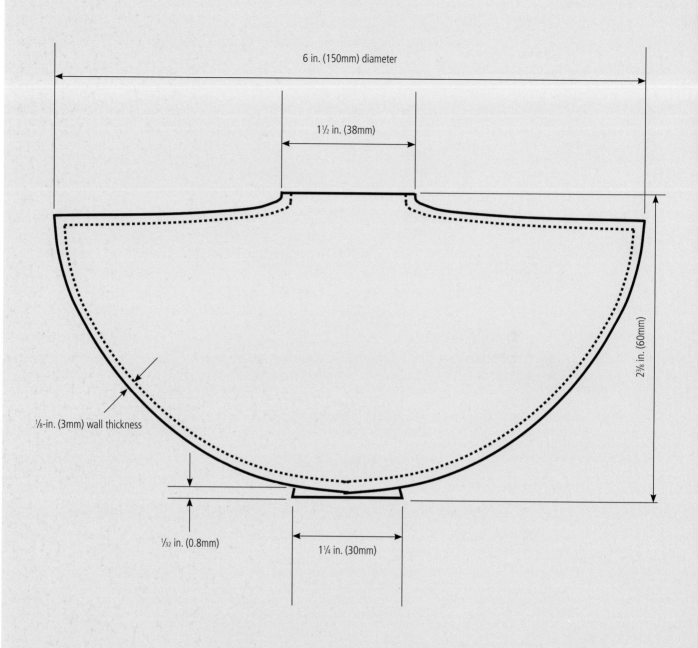

6 in. (150mm) diameter

1½ in. (38mm)

2³⁄₈ in. (60mm)

⅛-in. (3mm) wall thickness

¹⁄₃₂ in. (0.8mm)

1¼ in. (30mm)

TOOLS AND MATERIALS

- 1 x pre-seasoned cross-grain blank of European walnut *(Juglans regia)*, 3 in. (75mm) length x 6 in. (150mm) diameter
- ³⁄₈-in. (10mm) bowl gouge with long grind ● ³⁄₈-in. (10mm) spindle gouge ● 1-in. (25mm) square-end scraper
- 1-in. (25mm) round-nose scraper ● ½-in. (12mm) skew ● ½-in. (12mm) hollowing tool with scraping tip
- Small scraping attachment for hollowing tool ● ¼-in. (6mm) point tool

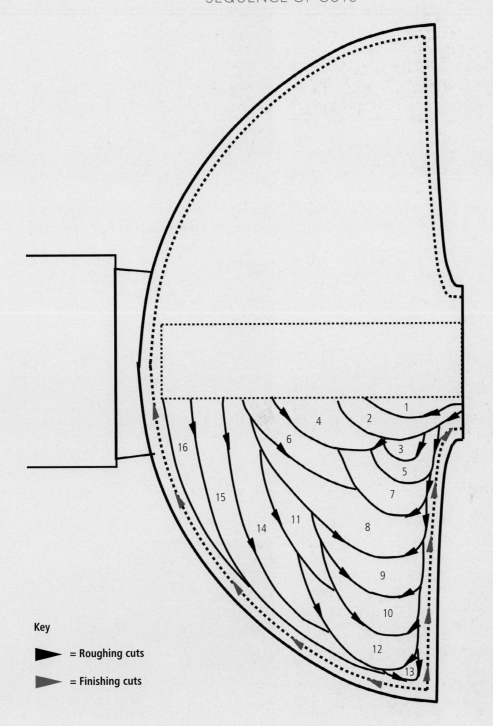

Key

▶ = Roughing cuts

▶ = Finishing cuts

SUPPLEMENTARY TOOLS AND SUNDRIES

• 8-in. (200mm)-diameter open-weave buffing pad and arbor • Buffing compound • Sanding sealer

• Your preferred wax • Power carver • Fine-tooth draw saw or similar

• Homemade sanding arbor for finishing the inside • Abrasives from 120 to 320 grit

• 1-in. (25mm) sawtooth drill bit • Calipers • Sanding arbor • Drill-bit extension • Battery-powered drill

1 Mount the blank via the chuck on a ³⁄₈-in. (10mm) screw chuck, bringing up the tail center for added security and support. Using a ³⁄₈-in. (10mm) bowl gouge, balance the outside of the blank.

2 Using a ³⁄₈-in. (10mm) bowl gouge, clean up the front face with a pull cut. Produce a tenon to suit the jaws of your chuck and a waste area approximately ³⁄₈ in. (10mm) wide.

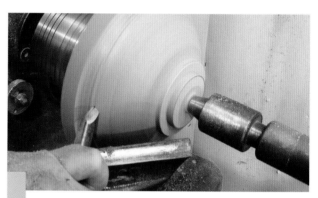

3 Using a ½-in. (12mm) skew chisel, refine the profile of the tenon to match the chuck jaw profile. Here the tool is horizontal on the tool rest with the tip trailing in a scraping mode.

4 Using a ³⁄₈-in. (10mm) bowl gouge, produce the base profile from the waste area to the shoulder with pull cuts. Working from the base out, aim for one continuous curve.

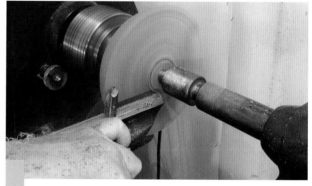

5 Use a 1-in. (25mm) square-end scraper to refine the surface, again working from inside out.

6 Reverse the form into the jaws, bringing up the center for support. Clean up the front face with pull cuts using a ³⁄₈-in. (10mm) bowl gouge. Mark the diameter of the rim onto the front face using a pencil and rule; from this, produce the top profile, working out to produce a flowing, single-curved top section. Take small cuts here and check the flow of the line from the rim outward, as any change in direction will be obvious.

7 Using a 1-in. (25mm) round-nose scraper, refine the top surface, working from the inside out.

8 The edge at the shoulder will be extremely sharp; if touched when spinning it will easily cut your hand. Radius this edge slightly with 180-grit abrasive to prevent injury.

9 Measure the height of the form from the base to the top of the rim. Subtract ⅜ in. (10mm) from this and transfer this measurement to the shaft of a 1-in. (25mm) sawtooth drill bit with a permanent marker, then drill out the form to this line.

10 Using a ½-in. (12mm)-diameter articulated hollowing tool with a small scraping tip, open out the hole to the rim following the sequence of cuts in the diagram on page 129.

11 Once the diameter at the entrance has been established, continue to work back into the form, replicating the top profile. The wall thickness is not critical with a seasoned blank, but my own preference is for the weight to complement the form, so here it was turned to ⅛ in. (3mm). You can see here that the cutter has been articulated to reach under the shoulder, with the tool handle rotated counter-clockwise slightly to trail the cutting tip. This lessens the twisting forces on the tool, making the cut more controllable. The cutter is pushed into the undercut a short way into the form, arcing into the form opening to further open out the inside.

12 When hollowing a much larger form of the same profile, the cutter has to be articulated farther around, allowing the cutting edge to be correctly presented to the wood to cut. The twisting forces on the tool when this is done multiply the farther into the form you cut. To prevent catching, rotate the tool farther counter-clockwise until you find the cut easy to control. The cutter can then reach the shoulder comfortably. The picture here shows this in a similar form with the sides cut away.

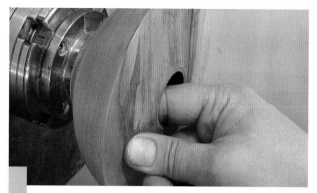

13 Check the depth you have cut under the shoulder regularly, as with this form it is easy to cut through the edge. To do this on a small form, simply use your thumb and forefinger to check the wall thickness.

14 Continue hollowing down into the form, flowing out from the base from the fulcrum of the tool and tool rest. While this breaks the rules of cutting with supported grain, at this stage we are removing only the unwanted waste material. Check the wall thickness down to the base using calipers. On deeper forms, a depth gauge can be used as calipers will not reach.

15 Finish the inside from 100- to 240-grit abrasive. To do this I have cut down an old sanding arbor so it fits through the entrance hole. The arbor is held in a standard drill-bit extension, which in turn is tightened into a battery-powered drill.

16 Rest the extension onto the tool rest, treating the sanding arbor as a scraper. Make sure it is abrading at center height and that the drill is held higher than the arbor, producing a trailing angle. Switch on the lathe to around 300 rpm, gently hold the extension and start the drill to a speed of around 800 rpm. You can then sand all the way around the inside of the form up to the shoulder. If you prefer, use a length of dowel with abrasive attached to the end instead.

17 Finish the undercut with abrasive: do not at any stage stick your fingers into a spinning hollow form. Using a homemade sanding arbor as in project 7 (see page 156), finish from 100 to 240 grit with the lathe speed set to around 500 rpm.

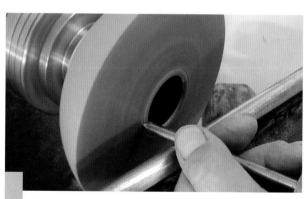

18 Use a ¼-in. (6mm) point tool to make a shallow groove to frame the rim.

19 Finish the outside with abrasive from 120 to 340 grit by hand or, if you prefer, power-sand with an arbor in a drill.

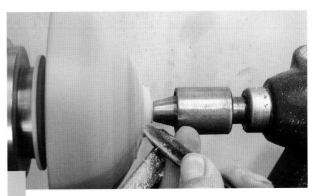

20 Reverse between a cone friction drive turned from a waste piece of wood, applying moderate pressure via the tail center. Use a ⅜-in. (10mm) bowl gouge to reduce the waste and produce the foot, in turn flowing from the foot outward to blend into the belly of the form previously shaped.

21 Reduce the waste further and concave the base using a ⅜-in. (10mm) spindle gouge.

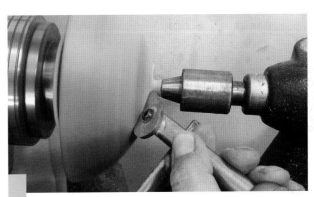

22 Refine the surface using a 1-in. (25mm) square-end scraper, working from the base out to the rim.

23 Finish the form from the base to shoulder with abrasive by hand from 120 to 340 grit.

24 Stop the lathe and cut through the remaining waste with a fine-bladed saw, taking care not to damage the rim of the base.

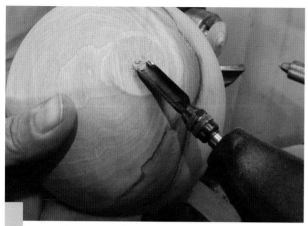

25 Remove any remaining waste carefully with a power carver or sharp chisel, always cutting away from your body.

26 Refine with 120-grit abrasive attached to a small sanding arbor set into a friction drive or a waste piece of wood in the chuck jaws. Alternatively, it can be held and driven in the headstock via a Jacobs chuck; if using this method, make sure the Jacobs chuck is secured with a draw bar to prevent it coming loose.

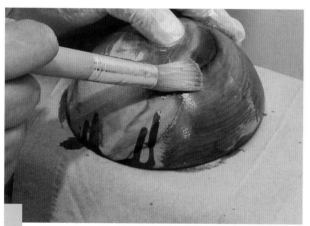

27 Apply several coats of sanding sealer, wiping away any excess, and allow to dry.

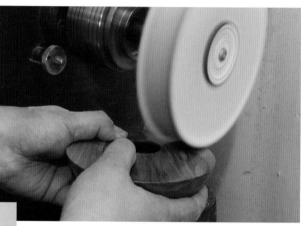

28 Once the sealer is fully dry, buff the form off the lathe using Tripoli brown compound as the wood is dark and open-grained (the white compound would be forced into the grain of the wood, ruining its appearance).

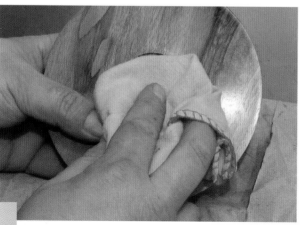

29 Apply several coats of wax off the lathe using a soft cloth, then dry and buff by hand with a clean cloth.

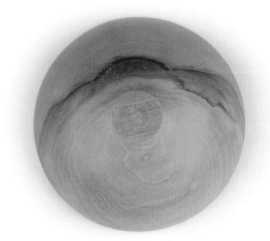

HANDY HINT
As with Project 3, Hollowed Form
Turned Through the Base (see page
106), it is important to present the
cutting tip of your hollowing tool
to trail when first contacting the
wood. This is especially important
in producing a form with such a
steep undercut. Get into the habit
of marking the tool shaft with a
permanent marker so that you can
confidently rotate the cutting tip
when out of view within the form
to trail prior to cutting.

This project shows you how to make a lidded form incorporating a metal bead and a free-form finial. The project uses seasoned yew for the main form with a contrasting wood (anjan) for the lid and finial. The form is turned end grain with the grain running parallel to the spindle axis of the lathe. For the main form, lid and finial size, I worked in thirds (see page 76): the base diameter is one-third of the form diameter; the external diameter of the lid is again one-third of the main form diameter; and the finial height is half of the height of the form (including the bead).

PROJECT SIX

LIDDED FORM
WITH FINIAL

LIDDED FORM WITH FINIAL

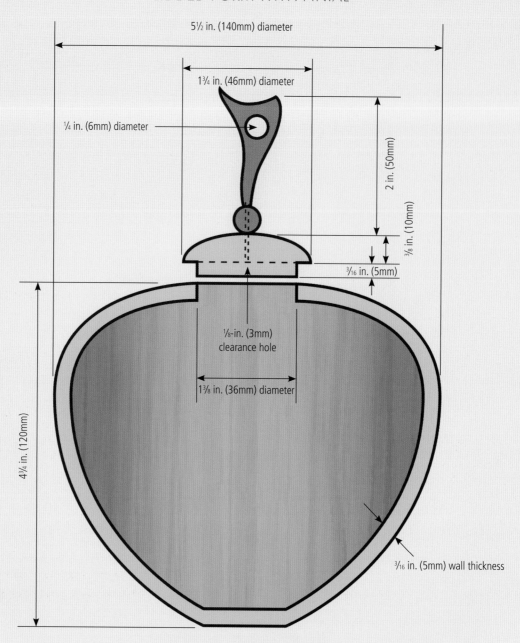

5½ in. (140mm) diameter

1¾ in. (46mm) diameter

¼ in. (6mm) diameter

2 in. (50mm)

⅜ in. (10mm)

³⁄₁₆ in. (5mm)

⅛-in. (3mm) clearance hole

1⅜ in. (36mm) diameter

4¾ in. (120mm)

³⁄₁₆ in. (5mm) wall thickness

TOOLS AND MATERIALS

- 1 x seasoned piece of yew *(Taxus baccata)* 6¾ in. (170mm) length x 8 in. (200mm) diameter
- 1 x piece of anjan *(Hardwickia binata)*; lid 1³¹⁄₃₂-in. (50mm)-square x 3⁵⁄₃₂-in. (80 mm) parallel-grain blank;
  finial 3⁵⁄₃₂-(80 mm) x 1³⁷⁄₆₄-(40mm) x 2⁵⁄₆₄-in. (10mm) parallel-grain blank • ½-in. (12mm) bowl gouge
- ⅜-in. (10mm) spindle gouge • ½-in. (12mm) skew chisel • ¼-in. (6mm) parting tool • ⅛-in. (3mm) parting tool
- 1-in. (25mm) square-end scraper • Tipped shear scraper, cranked ⅝-in. (16mm) Kelton hollower • 1-in. (25mm) skew chisel

SUPPLEMENTARY TOOLS AND SUNDRIES

- 1 x wood screw 1-in. (25mm) length x ⅛ in. (3mm) diameter • 1-in. (25mm) sawtooth bit • Jacobs chuck
- Hook-and-loop abrasives from 120–600 grit • Sanding arbor • Paper towel • Cellulose sanding sealer • Fine-tooth saw blade
- Your preferred wax • Vernier calipers • ⅛-in. (3mm) drill • PVA glue • ⁵⁄₁₆-in. (8mm) drill • 8-in. (200mm) buffing wheel
- Fine-point awl • Wire cutter • Medium-viscosity CA glue • Latex gloves • High-viscosity CA glue

1 Mark both ends of the blank and place between centers. Use a ½-in. (12mm) bowl gouge and rough down to the round, taking into account a suitable speed for your lathe and the size of blank used.

2 Use the ½-in. (12mm) bowl gouge to clean up the front face of the blank, turning in toward the revolving center from the external diameter.

HANDY HINTS

If you find the lid gets stuck in the jam chuck, use a screw in the center hole to gently remove it.

A ⅛-in. (3mm) drill is used to drill a clearance hole to take the wood screw. Make a small handle and glue a spare drill so you can drill out by hand. Using a Jacobs chuck saves time and can be kept handy for regular use.

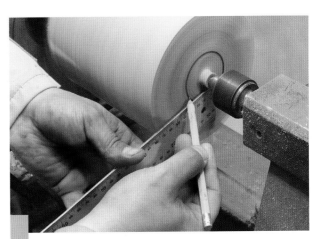

3 Mark on the front face the diameter of the tenon to suit your chuck jaws. Do this by using a rule and pencil with a low spindle rpm.

4 Using the ½-in. (12mm) bowl gouge, turn to this line and produce a tenon to the correct length to suit the chuck jaws. True up the tenon using a ½-in. (12mm) skew chisel held horizontal on the tool rest in a trailing mode.

5 Mark one-third of the way down from the top of the blank the center of the shoulder for the form. Turn the profile toward the base from this line.

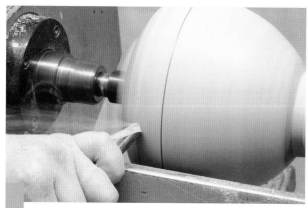

6 Using a ½-in. (12mm) bowl gouge, blend from the shoulder toward the headstock. Produce the shape for the top of the form in toward the drive center to a safe distance.

7 Reverse the form into the chuck and bring up the revolving center to centralize the form before tightening. Use the ½-in. (12mm) bowl gouge to clean up the front face and mark the external diameter of the neck using a pencil and rule, as before. Turn up to this line, producing a small shoulder of ⁵⁄₆₄ in.–⅛ in. (2–3mm) in height.

8 Using a 1-in. (25mm) square-end scraper, scrape the outside profile of the form to remove any tool marks.

9 Using a 1-in. (25mm) sawtooth bit in a Jacobs chuck, drill out the form to depth. Measure the height of the form and mark this on the bit – minus ⅜ in. (10mm) – using a marker. Withdraw the bit regularly to remove the shavings and to prevent binding.

10 Hollow the form by first opening the entrance hole to the previously marked line. Work from the shoulder down toward the base and use calipers to measure the wall thickness regularly, aiming for a wall thickness of ³⁄₁₆–¼ in. (5–6mm).

11 Check the depth with a depth gauge before finishing, taking a measurement from inside and comparing to the outside base line. Finish with the hollowers, leaving the base around ⁵⁄₁₆ in. (8mm) thick. The base will be slightly concaved later to allow the form to sit properly, thus removing some of this thickness.

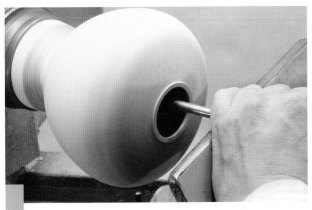

12 Using a tipped scraping tool, shear-scrape the inside profile to a good finish.

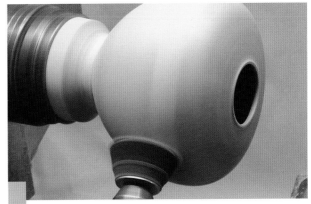

13 Finish the outside using hook-and-loop abrasive on a 2-in. (50mm) sanding arbor in a power drill from 120 to 400 grit. Dampen the surface with a small amount of water on a paper towel and cut back with 600-grit abrasive once dry.

HANDY HINT

To achieve a good fit for the lid, finish the form and lid so the lid fit is slightly tighter than that required. Once finished, the entrance hole in the main form can be refined to the exact size of the lid by using 600-grit abrasive inside the hole until a good fit is achieved. All that is needed then is to apply the wax finish to this and finally to buff with a cloth.

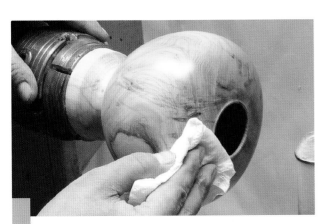

14 Apply several coats of sanding sealer, removing any excess with a cloth. If required, cut back with a 600-grit abrasive by hand. Buff the form with the lathe speed set around 1,000 rpm with a cloth. Alternatively, the whole form can be buffed using a buffing system when completed.

15 Use a friction drive in the chuck made from waste wood to fit the opening of the form. Protect the form by placing a towel over the drive and bring up the revolving center. Using a ³⁄₈-in. (10mm) spindle gouge, refine the base profile and turn down the waste material to a diameter of ³⁄₈ in. (10mm). Concave the base and blend the profile. Clean up with the 1-in. (25mm) scraper. Finish with 120–600-grit abrasive and apply sanding sealer and buff, as before. With the lathe stationary, cut the waste material from the base using a fine saw blade. Remove the remaining waste using a sharp chisel or reciprocal carver and blend with abrasive. Finish as before with sanding sealer, then apply your chosen wax and buff by hand.

MAKING THE LID

16   Rough the blank so that the outside diameter is larger than the shoulder of the main form. Turn a tenon on one end to fit the chuck jaws and tighten into the chuck. Clean up the front face using a ³⁄₈-in. (10mm) spindle gouge to remove the center mark.

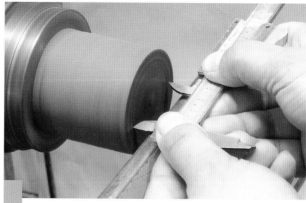

17   Using vernier calipers, measure the internal diameter of the neck in the form. Transfer this measurement to the front face of the blank. Only allow the left tip of the vernier calipers to contact the wood while trailing the tip.

18   Use a ¼-in. (6mm) parting tool to part up just short of this line, making the shoulder approximately ³⁄₁₆ in. (5mm) wide.

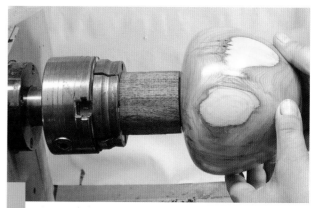

19   Offer the form up to the lid and continue to remove small amounts of material with the ¼-in. (6mm) parting tool until a good fit is achieved.

20   Measure the outside neck diameter of the hollow form and mark, as before, onto the base of the lid. Using the ¼-in. (6mm) parting tool, part down short of this line, making it approximately ³⁄₁₆ in. (5mm) wide. Offer the form up onto the lid and continue to remove small amounts of material until the external diameter of the lid matches that of the neck.

21   Using the ¼-in. (6mm) parting tool, produce a recess approximately ¼ in. (6mm) deep x ½ in. (12mm) diameter in the base. Once complete, rotate the parting tool counter-clockwise and use it to slightly scrape or round over the edge of the recess.

22 Use a 1-in. (25mm) skew chisel horizontally on the tool rest in a trailing mode to produce a countersink in the center of the recess to take the head of the wood screw. In this instance, the depth will be ¼ in. (6mm) in diameter x ⅛ in. (3mm).

23 Using the skew in a scraping, slightly trailing, mode, produce several beads on the base using the toe.

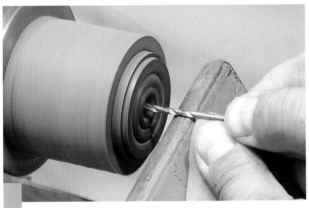

24 Use a ⅛-in. (3mm) drill to drill a central hole approximately ¾ in. (20mm) deep, so that when the lid is parted off the hole goes all the way through.

25 Finish the base with 240-grit abrasive by hand down to 400 grit. Clean up the outside diameter of the lid lightly with 320–400 grit. Regularly check that the form has a good fit.

HANDY HINT

You can make several lids at a time that can then be used later for similar-sized forms. Just make the base of the lid to finish, but part off thicker to allow the top to be shaped later. To do this, just turn the hole in the form to fit the lid instead of the other way round.

26 Apply cellulose sanding sealer, allow to dry and buff back with a towel with the lathe set to 1,500 rpm.

27 Using a ⅛-in. (3mm) parting tool, part into the lid, leaving it about ¾ in. (20mm) thick to allow for the forming of the top profile. Stop the lathe prior to parting all the way through and cut off the lid with a fine saw blade.

28 Turn a jam chuck to fit the lid into. Use a ⅜-in. (10mm) spindle gouge to turn the top profile of the lid. Take the lid out regularly to check the profile by placing it into the form. Turn your desired profile to finish.

29 Once complete, finish to 600 grit as before. Apply sanding sealer and buff with a towel with the lathe speed running around 1,500 rpm. At this stage you can apply your chosen wax/finish if desired. The lid is now completed with the addition of a small contrasting button, which will be placed into the base of the form to cover the screw head.

MAKING THE FINIAL

30 Draw the desired finial shape onto a piece of paper and stick this to the wood using PVA glue. Alternatively, the design can be drawn directly onto the wood. Use a scroll saw, or cut out by hand using a coping saw. Cut slightly outside of the line, as the shape can be refined later.

31 Use a suitable diameter drill – in this case 5⁄16 in. (8mm) – to drill out the circle area. A low-speed hand-held power drill or a drill press can be used.

32 Shape and blend the outside of the finial using 120 grit held on a 2-in. (50mm) hook-and-loop arbor in a Jacobs chuck in the headstock of the lathe. Once the main blending has been achieved, finish by hand using 120 down to 600 grit. Blend the inside of the hole again by hand, either rolling up the abrasive into a tight tube or wrapping it around a small file.

33 Once complete, apply sanding sealer and buff using a soft 8-in. (200mm) buffing wheel. Alternatively, buff by hand using a soft cloth when dry.

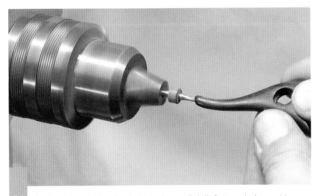

34 Again, using the Jacobs chuck and a small drill, first mark the position for the hole using a fine-point awl and, in this case, using a $\frac{5}{64}$-in. (2mm) drill. Drill out a hole $\frac{3}{16}$ in. (5mm) deep while holding the finial up to the drill and pushing onto the drill.

35 Dry-assemble the screw through the base of the lid and bead. Cut the screw off to length so that around $\frac{5}{32}$ in. (4mm) is protruding out from the bead – use a large set of wire cutters for this. Alternatively, cut the screw in a vice with a fine hacksaw. Drip medium-viscosity CA glue into the hole of the finial and screw the lid, bead and finial together. Align the finial so that it runs in line with the grain of the lid and allow to dry.

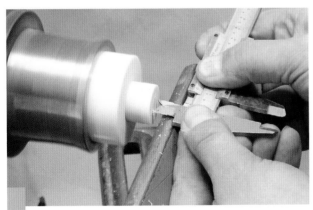

36 Turn a small button to fit inside the recess of the base in the lid to cover the screw head with alternative material or contrasting wood. Prepare the button material to fit into the jaws of the chuck. Clean up the front face using a $\frac{1}{4}$-in. (6mm) parting tool. Rough down a section of the material and mark the diameter of the recess onto this face with vernier calipers, as before.

37 Using a $\frac{1}{4}$-in. (6mm) parting tool, part down to this mark, checking for a good fit into the lid as you proceed.

38 Using the ¼-in. (6mm) parting tool, slightly roll the tool counter-clockwise. Use the burr of the edge as a scraper to slightly dome the front of the button.

39 Measure the depth of the recess and mark this for the thickness of the button using a pencil. Part off the button using a ⅛-in. (3mm) parting tool. Part in until a small amount of material is left and cut off using a fine saw blade. Place a small piece of abrasive on a flat surface and rub the back of the button flat. Drip a small amount of high-viscosity CA glue into the recess around the screw head and material. Push the button into the base. Be careful not to use too much glue or it can squeeze out and stick to your fingers. Wear latex-type gloves when doing this in case of any overspill. The lid is now fully complete. Apply wax to the lid and finial, then buff by hand.

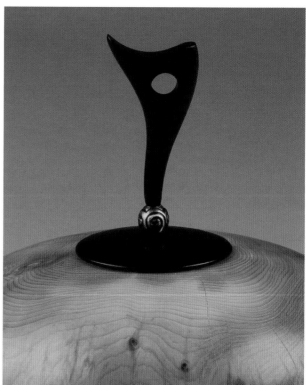

In this project, a thin-walled hollow form is turned, finished and seasoned. The wood used is beech, with the blank cut from a large log to exclude the pith and the grain aligned parallel to the spindle axis of the lathe for turning. Forms with a small entrance hole are seen as the most difficult type to turn because tool access and view into the form are greatly reduced. A good way to practice these forms is to start by producing forms that have a larger entrance hole. Once you have the hang of these, you can gradually reduce the diameter of the hole.

PROJECT SEVEN
THIN-WALLED HOLLOW FORM

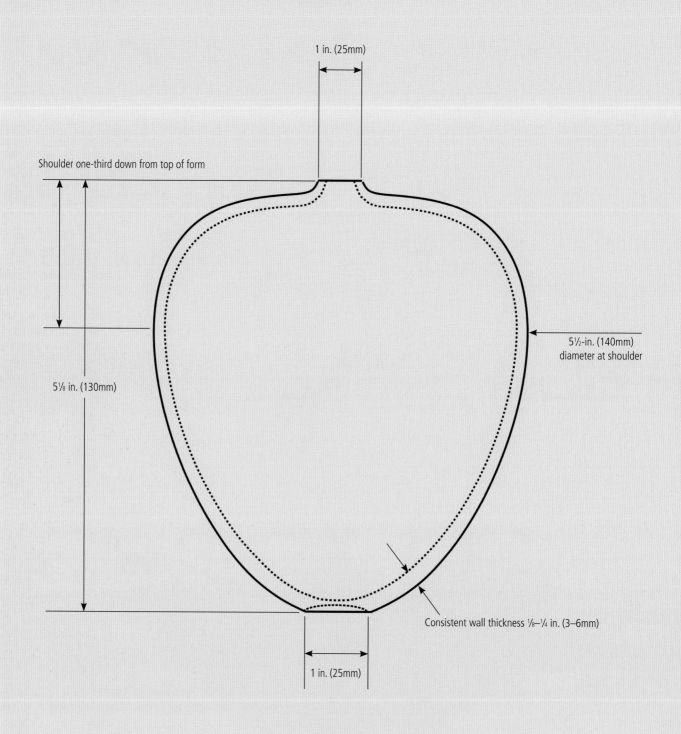

1 in. (25mm)

Shoulder one-third down from top of form

5½-in. (140mm)
diameter at shoulder

5⅛ in. (130mm)

Consistent wall thickness ⅛–¼ in. (3–6mm)

1 in. (25mm)

TOOLS AND MATERIALS

- 1 x unseasoned piece of spalted beech *(Fagus sylvatica)*, 6 in. (150mm) length x 8 in. (200mm) diameter
- 1-in. (25mm) spindle roughing gouge ● ⅜-in. (10mm) bowl gouge ● ¼-in. (6mm) spindle gouge
- 1-in. (25mm) square-end scraper ● ½-in. (12mm) skew ● ¼-in. (6mm) parting tool
- ½-in. (12mm) hollowing tool with scraping tip ● Small scraping attachment for hollowing tool

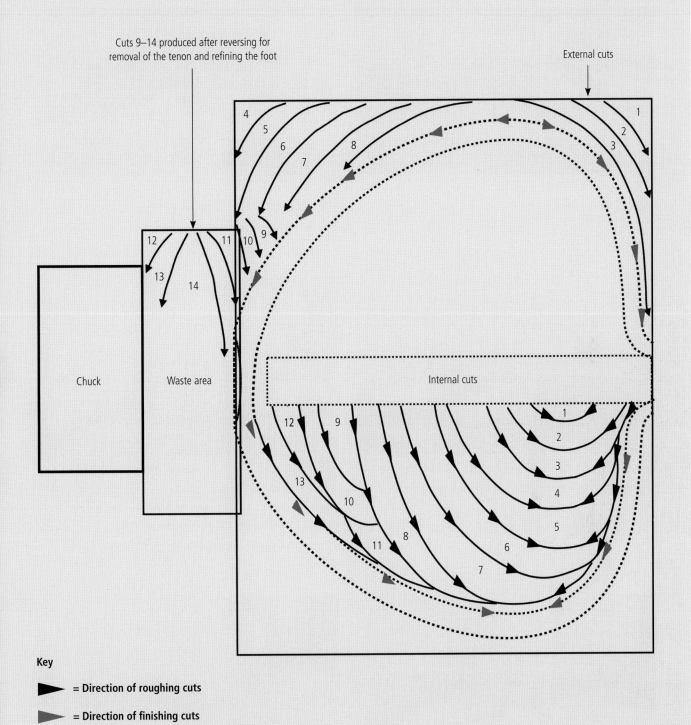

Cuts 9–14 produced after reversing for removal of the tenon and refining the foot

External cuts

Chuck

Waste area

Internal cuts

Key

= Direction of roughing cuts

= Direction of finishing cuts

SUPPLEMENTARY TOOLS AND SUNDRIES

• Lemon oil • Finishing oil • 8-in. (200mm)-diameter open-weave buffing pad and arbor
• Buffing compound • Power carver • Fine-tooth draw saw or similar • Jacobs chuck • ⅝-in. (15mm) drill bit
• Homemade sanding arbor for finishing the inside • Abrasives from 120 to 320 grit • Wax or desired finish

1 Mount the blank between centers. Using a 1-in. (25mm) spindle roughing gouge, rough to the round.

2 Using a ⅜-in. (10mm) bowl gouge, clean up the base to produce a tenon to suit the jaws of your chuck and produce a waste area approximately 1 in. (25mm) wide, the shoulder of which sits against the front of the chuck jaws.

3 Using a ½-in. (12mm) skew chisel, refine the profile of the tenon to match the chuck jaw profile. Here the tool is horizontal on the tool rest with the tip trailing in a scraping mode.

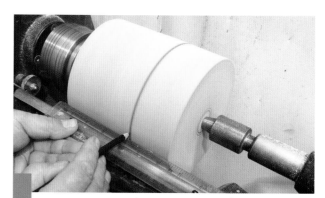

4 Reverse the blank and tighten into the jaws. Bring up the tail center and clean up the front face of the blank using a ⅜-in. (10mm) bowl gouge, stopping a safe distance from the tail center. Mark the position of the shoulder – in this case, two-thirds of the height of the blank, excluding the tenon. Mark the diameter of the opening and the outside rim on to the front face.

5 Using a ⅜-in. (10mm) bowl gouge, turn the profile for the top of the form, working downhill from the shoulder toward the rim. Aim for one continuous flowing line, refining as you go.

6 Continue with the ⅜-in. (10mm) bowl gouge and produce the profile below the shoulder toward the base. Do not at this stage reduce the material at the base less than half of the diameter – you need to maintain rigidity for the hollowing process later.

7 Measure the height of the form from the base to rim. Subtract ⅜ in. (10mm) and mark this measurement onto the shaft of a ⅝-in. (15mm)-long drill held in a Jacobs chuck and tailstock. Drill to depth using the mark as a reference; remove the cutter regularly to clear any shavings and prevent the drill from binding.

8 Using a ½-in. (12mm)-diameter shaft hollowing tool with a shielded ring-type cutter, hollow the top third of the form following the sequence shown in the diagram on page 151. Work from inside of the drilled hole out in small arcs using the intersection of the tool and tool rest as a fulcrum. Make sure the tool cutter is trailing, with the handle slightly raised above center to achieve this.

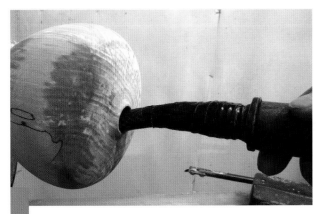

9 Work down inside the form in stages, removing the shavings as you progress to prevent the tool binding. Here a small homemade hose attachment is used with a workshop vacuum to suck out the waste. The wall should be turned to a consistent thickness of ⅛–¼ in. (3–6mm), starting from the rim as you work down. If you hollow to a wall thickness of ¼ in. (6mm), this must be maintained throughout the whole form.

At this stage, you may decide to rough-turn the form for finishing later after seasoning – if, for instance, you want to add a lid that will require the wood to be stable. To rough-turn, produce the wall to ½ in. (12mm) thickness, taking the form to step 20, and then season as per the instructions on page 38. The method for remounting and finishing after seasoning is shown at the end of this project (steps 30–36).

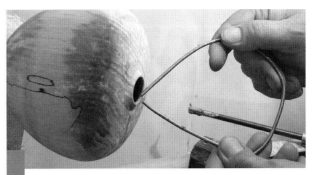

10 Checking the thickness of the wall at the top of the form can be difficult due to the restricted angle and size of opening unless you have specialized calipers. A much simpler and cheaper way of measuring is to use a bent piece of wire. Take a rigid piece of wire and bend it to shape as in the picture; the gap between the two ends represents your desired wall thickness.

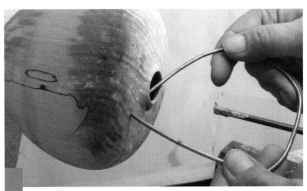

11 Feed one section of wire into the rim. If it rubs tightly on both sides, the wall is thicker than the gap between the ends of the wire. Refine further with the hollowing tool until the wire lightly touches both sides, checking farther into the form and refining with the hollowing tool as you proceed. In this picture, you can see the moisture of the form; before hollowing further, I decided to apply several coats of thin finishing oil, as the wood in the walls was starting to dry out.

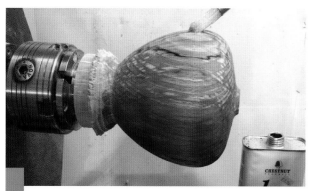

12 If the moisture within the wood fibers is allowed to escape too rapidly, the wood structure can fail, with cracks appearing. Applying thin oil helps to maintain the moisture within the wood by slowing down its release. This is particularly important when turning freshly felled wood, as the fibers will be far more susceptible to rapid moisture loss. In this instance, I use a brush to dampen the form with water. Take care when applying any liquids on the lathe that they do not come into contact with the electrics.

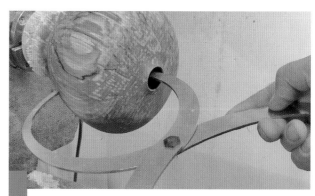

13 Continue hollowing, checking the wall thickness regularly with calipers as you proceed deeper.

14 On attaining the final depth indicated by reaching the bottom of the drilled hole, check with a depth gauge, offering up the measurement to the outside using a straight edge perpendicular to the base to see how much more has to be removed. Continue to depth, remembering that an extra ⅜-in. (10mm) thickness was left as a safety gap. Keep checking with the gauge after each refining cut until you reach the final required depth.

15 Finish the outside of the form with abrasive by hand from 120 to 320 grit. Keep the abrasive moving over the surface to prevent radial marks being induced on the surface. Use suitable air extraction and personal protective equipment when finishing with abrasive. Apply more coats of oil during finishing to keep the surface saturated.

16 If access can be safely gained to the inside, refine with a small round-profile scraper. Often hollowing tools come with finishing scrapers as an additional attachment, as shown in the one here. Take fine cuts to refine the surface. As with all scrapers, make sure the cutting edge is trailing.

17 Finish the undercut with abrasive. Here I used a homemade tool made from a bent welding rod wrapped in duct tape, with a thin strip of abrasive stuck to the end. The wire can be bent to the desired shape for accessing the undercut. Finish from 120 to 240 grit, with the lathe speed set to around 500 rpm.

18 Use a suitable length dowel with abrasive fixed to the end to finish deeper into the form.

19 Reverse the form between a cone friction drive turned from waste wood and the tail center. Make sure you apply only moderate pressure to avoid fracturing the rim.

20 Using a ⅜-in. (10mm) bowl gouge, reduce the tenon and waste area, blending the line of the form into the base.

21 Reduce the waste below the base further using a ¼-in. (6mm) spindle gouge. Undercut the base to produce a concave surface for the form to sit without rocking once completed.

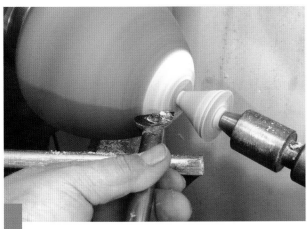

22 Refine the previously turned surface using a 1-in. (25mm) square-end scraper.

23 Using a ¼-in. (6mm) spindle gouge, finally reduce the waste to around ⅜ in. (10mm) diameter with the lathe speed set to 500 rpm.

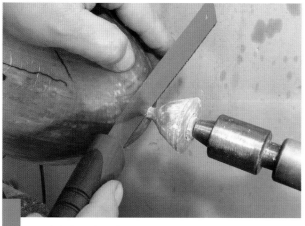

24 Stop the lathe and cut through the remaining waste with a fine-bladed saw, taking care not to damage the rim of the base.

25 Remove any remaining waste carefully with a power carver or sharp chisel, always cutting away from your body.

26 Refine with 120-grit abrasive attached to a small sanding arbor set into a friction drive or a waste piece of wood in the chuck jaws. Alternatively, it can be held and driven in the headstock via a Jacobs chuck. If using this method, make sure the Jacobs chuck is secured with a draw bar to prevent it coming loose.

27 Apply a final coat of lemon oil or finishing oil. Weigh the form, noting the date and weight, and season by placing into an open plastic bag following the instructions on page 38.

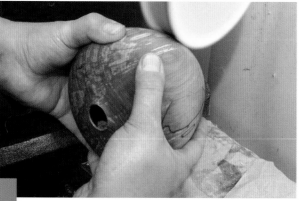

28 Once seasoned, I applied two coats of finishing oil and allowed the form to dry, after which it was buffed off the lathe.

29 Apply a final coat of finishing oil, wipe away the excess and, once dry, buff by hand with a soft cloth. The project is now finished.

30 Mount between a cone friction drive and tail center via the indent left in the base from the initial roughing process. Clean up the tenon and shoulder of the waste area using a ⅜-in. (10mm) bowl gouge. Refine the profile of the tenon with a ½-in. (12mm) skew in trailing mode as in step 3.

31 Reverse and tighten into the chuck. Refine the external profile of the form with a ⅜-in. (10mm) bowl gouge, working from the shoulder to the rim and then from the shoulder to the base.

32 Using a ¼-in. (6mm) spindle gouge with the flutes rotated 45° counter-clockwise, refine the opening to the round, cutting at around 10 o'clock with the tool edge trailing.

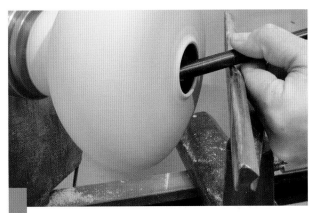

33 Hollow the inside as before, working down in stages. Refine with a scraping attachment and finish the inside with abrasive to 240 grit as shown in steps 17–18.

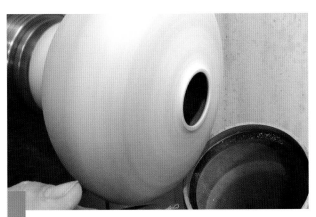

34 Finish the outside by hand with abrasive from 120 to 320 grit.

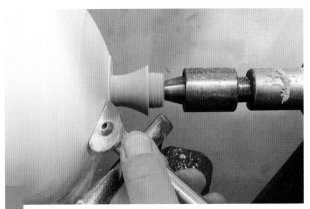

35 Reverse between a cone friction drive and the tail center, refine the base, scrape, finish and remove the waste section as shown in steps 23–26.

36 Buff the form off the lathe as in step 28. Apply your desired finish. I applied two coats of wax by hand. The form was then buffed to a soft sheen by hand using a soft cloth. The remounted maple form is now finished.

HANDY HINTS

Remember when hollowing with a scraping cutter that the cutting edge should be presented to cut on center and trailing, keeping the handle of the tool higher than the cutting tip to achieve this.

When turning thin-walled forms or roughing out forms from wood harvested from a recently felled tree, the moisture content will be high; this will be evident from the moisture that sprays out as it is turned at speed. In hot weather, keep the surfaces of the form damp by carefully applying water using a soft paintbrush. Take care not to get water into the electrics of the lathe; cover these areas first with plastic bags or sheets, or apply thin finishing oil.

GLOSSARY

Bark The protective outer layer of the tree's trunk, including the inner living bark and the outer dead bark.

Bead Rounded convex feature on a piece of turning, usually semicircular but may be more pointed.

Between centers The distance between the drive and tailstock center points.

Bevel The area immediately behind the cutting edge of the tool, which may be flat, hollow or convex.

Blank A prepared piece of lumber for turning. Long, thin pieces are normally referred to as spindle blanks, squat circular pieces are termed bowl blanks.

Board A piece of lumber with wane on at least one of the edges.

Catch Chance contact between the revolving workpiece and the tool edge, usually leading to damage to the workpiece.

Centers Provide drive and support for long, thin workpieces when held between the headstock and tailstock.

Checks A lengthwise separation of wood cells along the grain as a result of uneven shrinkage, commonly seen on end-grain surfaces.

Cove Rounded concave feature on a piece of turning.

Deciduous A type of tree where the leaves fall off after the yearly growth cycle, typical of most hardwoods, but not all.

Density The weight of wood substance per unit volume.

Drive center Pronged center on a Morse taper that fits into the headstock to provide drive to the work. Normally two or four pronged.

End grain The cross-sectional surface of a board.

Evergreen Tree or bush that has green leaves all through the year.

Faceplate Used to hold work to the headstock when it is impractical to support it with the tailstock.

Flute U-shaped depression along the inside of gouges.

Grain The direction of the wood fibers relative to the long axis of the tree trunk.

Grit A system of classifying the particle size on abrasive materials. The lower the number, the coarser the grit.

Hardwood Wood cut from broadleaved trees in the botanical group called angiosperms.

Headstock The main part of the lathe containing the drive shaft, motor and speed-change mechanism.

Heartwood Lumber from the central portion of the trunk; often darker due to the deposition of extractives.

Hygroscopic Having the ability to absorb water.

Moisture content The weight of water in a piece of lumber expressed as a percentage of the dry weight.

Morse taper A universal system for attaching accessories using push-fit tapers. Used in both the headstock and tailstock for the centers and other accessories such as drill chucks and boring bits.

Pith The small, soft and spongy core at the very center of the tree. May be hollow in some species.

Revolving center A tailstock center fitted with bearings so that it revolves with the lumber and eliminates any chance of burning the work.

Ring The layer of wood that a tree gains in a single year, made up of a band of earlywood and a band of latewood.

Sapwood The active lumber comprised of the most recent annual rings; it is usually lighter-colored than the heartwood.

Seasoning The process of drying wood to a usable state.

Shrinkage The changes in dimension that occur in a piece of wood as it dries below the fiber saturation point.

Softwood Wood from coniferous trees in the botanical group called gymnosperms.

Spalted Partially rotten wood that exhibits highly decorative coloration due to the fungal zone lines.

Split Separation of the wood tissue that extends completely through a board, usually on the end.

Tailstock The opposite end of the bed to the headstock, the tailstock moves along the length of the bed and houses an adjustable barrel for holding work between centers.

Tenon (or spigot) A dowel or pin on one end of a workpiece, usually used for jointing two pieces together or for holding by means of a chuck.

Tool rest A T-shaped rest for the cutting tools that fits into the banjo.

Trunk The main section of the tree producing the bulk of the lumber.

CONVERSION CHART

INCHES	CENTIMETERS	MILLIMETERS	INCHES	CENTIMETERS	MILLIMETERS
1/32	0.08	0.8	15/16	2.38	23.8
1/16	0.16	1.6	31/32	2.46	24.6
3/32	0.23	2.3	1	2.5	25
1/8	0.3	3	1 1/4	3.2	32
5/32	0.4	4	1 1/2	3.8	38
3/16	0.48	4.8	1 3/4	4.4	44
7/32	0.56	5.6	2	5.1	51
1/4	0.6	6	2 1/2	6.4	64
9/32	0.71	7.1	3	7.6	76
5/16	0.79	7.9	3 1/2	8.9	89
11/32	0.87	8.7	4	10.2	102
3/8	1.0	10	4 1/2	11.4	114
1/2	1.3	13	5	12.7	127
5/8	1.6	16	6	15.2	152
23/32	1.82	18.2	7	17.8	178
3/4	1.9	19	8	20.3	203
25/32	1.98	19.8	9	22.9	229
13/16	2.06	20.6	10	25.4	254
27/32	2.14	21.4	11	27.9	279
7/8	2.2	22	12	30.5	305
29/32	2.3	23			

The measurements in the projects have been rounded up for ease of use, and the chart above gives more detailed conversions from the imperial to the metric system. Conversions can introduce inaccuracies so I recommend you stick to one or the other and do not mix up measurements.

USEFUL WEBSITES

American Association of Woodturners (AAW)
www.woodturner.org

Ashley Iles
www.ashleyiles.co.uk

Association of Woodturners
of Great Britain (AWGB)
www.woodturners.co.uk

Axminster Tool Centre
www.axminster.co.uk

Crown Hand Tools
www.crownhandtools.ltd.uk

GMC Publications
www.thegmcgroup.com

Mark Sanger
www.marksanger.co.uk

Robert Sorby
www.robert-sorby.co.uk

Taunton Press
www.taunton.com

Henry Taylor
www.henrytaylortools.co.uk

The Tool Post
www.toolpost.co.uk

Woodland Trust
www.woodlandtrust.org.uk

Woodworkers Institute.com
www.woodworkersinstitute.com

BIBLIOGRAPHY

Baker, Mark, *Wood Turning: A Craftsman's Guide*. GMC Publications, 2012.

Baker, Mark, *Woodturning Projects*. GMC Publications, 2004.

Hayes, Derek, *Woodturning Design: Turning Inspiration into Form*. GMC Publications, 2011.

Hoadley, Bruce R., *Understanding Wood: A Craftsman's Guide to Wood Technology*. Taunton Press, 2000.

O'Donnell, Michael, *Turning Green Wood*. GMC Publications, 2000.

Porter, Terry, *Wood Identification and Use*. Revised and expanded edition, GMC Publications, 2007.

Rowley, Keith, *Woodturning: A Foundation Course*. GMC Publications, 1999.

ACKNOWLEDGMENTS

A big thank you to my good friend Mark Baker for his continued support of my work, and for his input, guidance and involvement in the construction of this, my first book. A big thank you to photographer Anthony Bailey for the exceptional amount of work and help in taking many of the pictures included within this book. Your assistance has been invaluable and is much appreciated.

Thank you to my friends George Foweraker and George Watkins for the supply of pictures of your work for inclusion and for your support of my work.

Thank you to my sponsors Crown Hand Tools Ltd, for their continued support and help.

IMAGE ACKNOWLEDGMENTS

Anthony Bailey pp. 2, 3, 5, 6, 11, 70, 72, 84, 87, 97, 99, 105, 107, 116, 117, 119, 125, 127, 135, 137, 146 bottom left and right, 147, 149, 158 top and bottom right, 159, 161, 163, 167, 168; Anthony Bailey/Mark Baker, GMC pp. 44, 45, 48–62, 64–69;

Carter Products p. 63 top left; Elbo Tools p. 63 bottom left; Lyle Jamieson p. 63 top right. Graphs on pp. 18, 19 by John Lovatt/Mark Baker. All other photos by Mark Sanger.

ABOUT THE AUTHOR

Mark's passion for working with wood started as a young boy, when he spent many happy hours with his grandfather making toys and other projects. On leaving school, Mark completed a four-year engineering apprenticeship in the aerospace industry. In 1993, he joined the police force and served for just under 12 years.

In 2000, while still working for the police, Mark decided he needed a hobby to relax, and took up woodturning. Soon this became a passion, a creative outlet and a hobby in which he could lose himself. He started showing his work in local galleries and, in 2004, decided to leave his career to pursue a full-time vocation working with wood.

Concentrating purely on gallery work, Mark had a chance meeting with Mark Baker, the editor of GMC's *Woodturning* magazine. This culminated in Mark writing the first of many articles on woodturning – something he continues to do today. Mark also teaches and demonstrates the craft in the UK and abroad; his work, which he sells via select galleries and direct commissions, includes pure turning as well as sculptural work influenced by his interest in Asian culture and philosophy.

When asked what lies at the center of his work, Mark replies: "Beginner's mind and the continual pursuit of refinement in everything I do."

SUPPLIERS

I have given contact details for suppliers and manufacturers whose products I have used in the book. There are many others that I do not have space to mention; you will find them in local directories and woodworking magazines.

UK

Ashley Iles (Edge Tools Ltd)
East Kirkby
Spilsby
Lincs PE23 4DD
Tel: +44 (0)1790 763372
www.ashleyiles.co.uk

Axminster Power Tool Centre
Unit 10
Weycroft Avenue
Axminster
Devon EX13 5PH
Tel: +44 (0)3332 406406
www.axminster.co.uk

Behlen Ltd
Unit 13
Peffermill Parc
25 King's Haugh
Edinburgh
EH16 5UY (by appointment only)
Tel: +44 (0)1316 616812
Toll-free (USA and Canada only): 1 866
785 7781 (non-European enquiries only)
www.behlen.co.uk

Chestnut Products
PO Box 536
Ipswich
IP4 5WN
Tel: +44 (0)1473 425878
www.chestnutproducts.co.uk

Crown Hand Tools Ltd
332–334 Coleford Road
Darnall
Sheffield S9 5PH
Tel: +44 (0)1142 612300
www.crownhandtools.com

General Finishes UK
Unit 13
Peffermill Parc
25 King's Haugh
Edinburgh EH16 5UY
(by appointment only)
Tel: +44 (0)1316 615553
www.generalfinishes.co.uk

Hamlet Craft Tools
The Forge
Peacock Estate
Livesey Street
Sheffield S6 2BL
Tel: +44 (0)1142 321338
www.hamletcrafttools.co.uk

Henry Taylor (Tools) Ltd
Peacock Estate
Livesey Street
Sheffield
S6 2BL
Tel: +44 (0)1142 340282/0321
www.henrytaylortools.co.uk

Liberon Waxes Ltd
Mountfield Industrial Estate
Learoyd Road
New Romney
Kent TN28 8XU
Tel: +44 (0)1797 367555
www.liberon.co.uk

Mylands
John Myland Ltd
26–34 Rothschild Street
London SE27 0HQ
Tel: +44 (0)208 6709161
www.mylands.co.uk

Peter Child
The Old Hyde
Little Yeldham Road
Little Yeldham
Nr Halstead
Essex CO9 4QT
Tel: +44 (0)1787 237291
www.peterchild.co.uk

Record Power Ltd
Unit B
Adelphi Way
Ireland Industrial Estate
Staveley
Chesterfield S43 3LS
Tel: +44 (0)1246 561520
www.recordpower.co.uk

Robert Sorby
Athol Road
Sheffield S8 0PA
Tel: +44 (0)1142 250700
www.robert-sorby.co.uk

Stiles & Bates
Upper Farm
Church Hill
Sutton
Dover
Kent CT15 5DF
Tel: +44 (0)1304 366360
www.stilesandbates.co.uk

The Tool Post
Unit 7, Hawksworth
Southmead Industrial Park
Didcot
Oxfordshire OX11 7HR
Tel: +44 (0)1235 511101
www.toolpost.co.uk

Turners Retreat
The Woodworkers Source
Snape Lane
Harworth
Notts DN11 8NE
Tel: +44 (0)1302 744344
www.turners-retreat.co.uk

Yandle & Sons Ltd
Hurst Works
Hurst
Martock
Somerset TA12 6JU
Tel: +44 (0)1935 822207
www.yandles.co.uk

AUSTRALIA

Vicmarc Machinery
52 Grice Street
Clontarf
Queensland 4019
Tel: +61 (0)7 3284 3103
www.vicmarc.com

CANADA

Oneway Manufacturing
Unit 1, 291 Griffith Road
Stratford
Ontario N5A 6S4
Tel: 1 519 271 7611
Toll-free (USA and Canada only):
1 800 565 7288
www.oneway.ca

Woodchucker's Supplies
Units 4 & 5
50 Venture Drive
Toronto
Ontario M1B 3L6
Toll-free (USA and Canada only):
1 800 551 0192
www.woodchuckers.com

NEW ZEALAND

Kelton Industries Ltd
PO Box 589
Kaitaia 500
Tel: +64 9 408 5862
www.kelton.co.nz

USA

Carter Products
2871 Northridge Drive
NW Grand Rapids
MI 49544
Tel: 1 888 622 7837
www.carterproducts.com

Craft Supplies USA
1287 E 1120 S
Provo, UT 84608
Tel: 1 800 551 8876
www.woodturnerscatalog.com

Elbo.com
6731 S. 66th E. Avenue
Tulsa
OK 74133
Tel: 1 918 492 8994
www.elbotool.com

General Finishes USA
2462 Corporate Circle
East Troy
WI 53120
Tel: 1 262 642 4545
Toll-free (USA and Canada only):
1 800 783 6050
www.generalfinishes.com

JT Turning Tools
LLC - 582 S. 126th Street
Omaha
NE 68154
Tel: 1 402 330 9801
www.jtturningtools.com

Lyle Jamieson
285 Lauri-Wil Lane
Traverse City
MI 49686
Tel: 1 231 947 2348
www.lylejamieson.com

Monster Lathe Tools
10102 W 13th St
Greeley
CO 80634
Tel: 1 970 301 4893
www.monster-lathe-tools.com

Packard Woodworks Inc
215 S Trade Street
Tryon
NC 28782
Tel: 1 828 859 6762
Toll-free (USA and Canada only):
1 800 683 8876
www.packardwoodworks.com

Thompson Lathe Tools
Doug Thompson
5479 Columbia Road
N. Olmsted
OH 44070
Tel: 1 440 241 6360
www.thompsonlathetools.com

Woodcraft Supply
LLC
PO Box 1686
Parkersburg
WV 26102-1686
Tel: 1 304 422 5412
Toll-free (USA and Canada only):
1 800 225 1153
www.woodcraft.com

INDEX

To order a book, or to request a catalog, contact:

The Taunton Press, Inc.

63 South Main Street, P.O. Box 5506, Newtown, CT 06470-5506

Tel: (800) 888-8286

www.tauntonstore.com